ANTIGUA ANI

TRAVEL GUIDE 2024

Paradise on Earth: A Guide to Antigua and Barbuda's Beauty

Andrea J. Armstrong

Copyright © Andrea J. Armstrong 2023

All right reserved. No part of this publication may be reproduced, distributed, or transmitted in any form or by any means, including photocopying, recording, or other electronic or mechanical methods, without the prior written permission of the publisher, except in the case of brief quotations embodied in critical reviews and certain other noncommercial uses permitted by copyright law.

TABLE OF CONTENT

CHAPTER 1 7
INTRODUCTION 7
    Welcome to Antigua and Barbuda 7
    15 Reasons to Book a Trip to Antigua and Barbuda 11
    An Overview of the History and Culture Of Antigua and Barbuda 16
    Geography and Climate of Antigua and Barbuda 21
    Arriving in Antigua and Barbuda 24
CHAPTER 2 27
ACCOMMODATION IN ANTIGUA 27
    5 Luxury Hotels 27
    5 Mid-Range Hotels 29
    Low-Cost Hotel 30
CHAPTER 3 33
ACCOMMODATION IN BARBUDA 33
    3 Luxury Hotel 33
    3 Mid-Range Hotel 34
    3 Low-Cost Hotel 35
CHAPTER 4 37
PLANNING YOUR TRIP 37
    Visa and Entry Requirements 37
    Travel Insurance 42

When to visit Antigua and Barbuda 44
CHAPTER 5 47
TOP 15 ATTRACTIONS IN ANTIGUA 47
Shirley Heights Lookout 47
Nelson's Dockyard 49
Devil's Bridge 52
Stingray City 54
Half Moon Bay 55
Darkwood Beach 58
Betty's Hope 60
Antigua Rainforest Canopy Tour 62
Cathedral of St. John the Divine 65
Museum of Antigua and Barbuda 67
Fort James 68
Hermitage Bay 70
Indian Town Point 72
Jolly Beach 74
Antigua Botanical Gardens 76
CHAPTER 6 79
TOP 10 ATTRACTIONS IN BARBUDA 79
Pink Sand Beach 79
Frigate Bird Sanctuary 81
Darby Cave 83

3

  Palmetto Point 84

  Buccaneer Beach 85

  Martello Tower 86

  Low Bay 87

  The Caves at Two Foot Bay 89

  Barbuda Council Museum 90

  The Highlands 91

CHAPTER 7 93

TRANSPORTATION AND GETTING AROUND 93

  Public Transportation 93

  Renting a Car 94

  Taxis 96

  Bicycle 97

  Ferries 98

  Private Yachts and Charter Boats 98

CHAPTER 8 101

OUTDOOR ACTIVITIES AND ADVENTURE 101

  Beaches in Antigua and Barbuda 101

  Water sports 106

  Hiking and Nature Excursions 109

  Golfing 111

CHAPTER 9 113

CULTURAL EXPERIENCES AND NIGHT LIFE 113

4

Annual Celebrations 113
Nightlife 116
CHAPTER 10 119
DINING AND CUISINE 119
  Local Food and Specialties 119
  Restaurants and Cafes 123
CHAPTER 11 127
SHOPPING AND SOUVENIRS 127
  Local Markets 127
  Handcrafted Goods 130
  Duty-Free Shopping 133
CHAPTER 12 137
PLANNING YOUR ITINERARY 137
  5 Days Itinerary 137
  7 Days Itinerary 140
CHAPTER 13 145
PRACTICAL INFORMATION 145
  Tourist Information Centers 145
  Emergency Contacts 146
  Local Etiquette and Customs 147
  Currency and Banking 149
  Language and Communication 150
  Packing Tips 151

Safety Tips	153
CHAPTER 14	155
CONCLUSION	155
Useful Phrases	155
Maps	157

CHAPTER 1

INTRODUCTION

Welcome to Antigua and Barbuda

As Linda stepped off the plane and onto the tarmac at V.C. Bird International Airport, she was met with the azure waters of the Caribbean. She had decided on the twin islands of Antigua and Barbuda as the perfect getaway from the hectic city life she had grown accustomed to. She could not help but feel an overwhelming sense of eagerness for the thrills and adventures that awaited her in this magnificent paradise as the warm tropical air caressed her face.

As soon as Linda arrived, she was greeted by the people's contagious grins and genuine hospitality. The kind and hospitable character of the people of Antigua and Barbuda reflected their status as a preferred vacation spot for those looking for a calm retreat in the Caribbean.

Linda traveled to the gorgeous beach side cottage she had picked as her lodging under the blazing sun. The Caribbean Sea's turquoise, crystal-clear seas met the pure white sand in the distance as seen from her balcony, which was nothing short of magnificent. It served as an invitation to travel and partake in the water activities for which the islands were famed.

She spent her first day lazing in the sunshine and enjoying the culinary treats of the local cuisine. Freshly caught fish, tropical fruits, and a range of regional specialties influenced by the islands' rich cultural heritage were all delicious to Linda. The cuisine was a tribute to Antigua and Barbuda's illustrious past, where West African, European, and Caribbean influences harmoniously coexisted to produce distinctive and delectable meals.

Linda's desire for exploration compelled her to take in all the islands' varied features. She went snorkeling and was amazed by the colorful coral reefs and the variety of marine life that lived below the water's surface. The islands' crystal-clear waters were an undersea paradise, teaming with diverse aquatic life and colorful fish.

A tour of the ancient English Harbour, home of Nelson's Dockyard, a UNESCO World Heritage Site, was one of the highlights of her trip. The impressive Georgian-era naval complex, which offered an insight into the islands' illustrious past as a significant British naval stronghold, astounded Linda.

Antigua & Barbuda also gave Linda the chance to unwind in beautiful surroundings, so it was not just about adventure and history. Each night, when she dozed off in the comfort of one of the opulent resorts that dot the islands' coastline, the sound of calm waves lapping at the shore served as her lullaby.

As Linda's trip to Antigua and Barbuda concluded, she became aware of how profoundly it had changed her. She left the jewel of the Caribbean with a heart full of memories, a soul fed by the kindness of the locals, and a spirit reignited by the splendor of nature. Linda will always have a particular place in her heart for Antigua & Barbuda as a result of her journey. There are times when solitude, getting outside, and experiencing other cultures may rejuvenate the soul.

15 Reasons to Book a Trip to Antigua and Barbuda

Here are 15 persuasive reasons to make this tropical paradise your next vacation destination:

1. **Pristine Beaches:** With their snow-white sand and crystal-clear waters, Antigua and Barbuda have some of the world's most stunning beaches.

2. **Ideal environment:** You may avoid harsh winters and take advantage of a consistently tropical environment thanks to the area's year-round warmth and sunshine.

3. **Abundant Coral Reefs**: The islands' abundant and well-maintained coral reefs provide fantastic snorkeling and diving opportunities.

4. **Water Sports:** The islands are a sanctuary for lovers of water sports, including windsurfing, kite surfing, and paddle boarding.

5. **Historical Sites:** Visit Nelson's Dockyard and other admirably preserved colonial-era locations to learn more about the area's rich past.

6. **Local celebrations and festivals:** Take part in community events like Carnival to fully experience the music and culture of the islands.

7. **Delectable Cuisine:** Experience the Caribbean's delights with fresh seafood, tropical fruits, and a blend of culinary influences.

8. **Warm-hearted Locals:** Visitors to Antigua and Barbuda are made to feel welcome and at home by the friendly locals that live there.

9. **Island hopping:** Antigua and Barbuda are close to other Caribbean islands, making day visits and exploration simple.

10. **Luxurious Resorts:** A variety of opulent resorts are available on the islands, making them ideal for lavish relaxation and pampering.

11. **Adventure Activities**: To discover the lush interior of the islands, go horseback riding, zip-lining, or hiking.

12. **Bird Watching:** One of the largest frigate bird sanctuaries in the world is located on Barbuda; it is a haven for bird watchers.

13. **Sailing:** Take part in one of the many regattas and sailing competitions while enjoying the excitement of sailing in the clear, tranquil waters of the Caribbean.

14. **Stunning Sunsets:** The Caribbean Sea sunsets are a sight to behold and make for the ideal setting for a romantic evening.

15. **Wellness & Spa Retreats:** Antigua and Barbuda have many resorts with top-notch spa and wellness amenities for relaxation and regeneration.

An Overview of the History and Culture Of Antigua and Barbuda

The twin-island nation of Antigua and Barbuda, which is situated in the Eastern Caribbean, has a rich history and a dynamic culture that are influenced by its native peoples, European colonizers, African heritage, and other groups. Let us explore this Caribbean treasure's fascinating history and culture.

HISTORY

Precolonial Period: The peaceful Arawak and Carib native peoples lived on the islands of Antigua and Barbuda before European explorers arrived. After the Caribs arrived after the Arawaks, there were confrontations between the two populations.

Christopher Columbus was the first European to colonize Antigua, doing so in 1493. Following British colonization of the islands in the 17th century, Barbuda and Redonda were later annexed. African slaves were imported to labor on the sugar plantations, which played a key part in the economy of the islands.

Emancipation and Independence: Antigua and Barbuda attained complete independence from the United Kingdom on November 1, 1981, after slavery was abolished in 1834. The culture and social dynamics of the islands are still influenced by colonization and slavery.

CULTURE

Music and Dance: Calypso, reggae, and soca are among the major musical genres in Antigua and Barbuda. The yearly Carnival on the islands, which features vibrant costumes, music, and dance, is well-known. Antigua's traditional "benna" music is an essential component of the community's culture.

Food: The delicious combination of African, European, and indigenous elements in Antigua and Barbuda's cuisine is evident. Seafood is a mainstay, while regional specialties include "ducana," a sweet potato dumpling, and "fungie and pepperpot," a cornmeal-based dish with a robust stew.

Language: Antigua and Barbuda's official language is English, reflecting its origins as a British colony. However, people on the islands frequently use Antiguan Creole, a distinctive synthesis of African, English, and other regional tongues.

Arts & crafts: There is a strong arts and crafts scene on the islands. Exquisite wood carvings, bright batik fabrics, and delicate pottery are all produced locally by craftsmen. The natural beauty and colorful culture of Antigua and Barbuda are reflected in the local art scene.

Festivals and Celebrations: The islands hold several cultural festivals all year long in addition to Carnival. The Antigua and Barbuda International Film Festival highlights both local and international talent while Antigua Sailing Week draws tourists from all over the world.

Religion: The bulk of the population is Christian, and the islands are home to several different denominations. The church has a big impact on people's social and cultural lives.

Heritage Locations: The islands are home to several historical locations, including as Nelson's Dockyard in

English Harbor, a significant naval base during the colonial era and a UNESCO World Heritage Site today.

The history and culture of Antigua and Barbuda are an enthralling fusion of native traditions, European colonial influences, African influences, and a distinctive Caribbean flair. Warm hospitality and the chance to immerse oneself in a complex tapestry of customs and experiences that have developed over ages are extended to visitors to these twin islands.

Geography and Climate of Antigua and Barbuda

Travelers find Antigua and Barbuda to be a desirable destination due to its distinctive terrain and tropical environment. Let us explore this fascinating country's geography and climate.

GEOGRAPHY

Two Islands: Antigua and Barbuda are made up of two main islands, as the name implies. The smaller of the two islands, Barbuda, is flatter and even smaller, with several lagoons and coral reefs encircling its coasts. Antigua, the larger of the two, is renowned for its comparatively flat landscape. The nation also includes the tiny, deserted island of Redonda.

The islands are endowed with a long coastline that is home to many stunning bays, coves, and beaches. Particularly in Antigua, visitors are drawn in large numbers by the island's immaculate white-sand beaches.

Topography: Low-lying limestone and coral formations define Antigua's landscape. Barbuda is a coral-based island that is flatter and has a spectacular lagoon known as the Codrington Lagoon.

CLIMATE

Antigua and Barbuda have a tropical marine climate, which implies that they get warm, comfortable weather all year long. Their placement in the Eastern Caribbean has an impact on the climate.

The islands experience a rainy season from June to November, with September often seeing the worst downpours. Brief but intense downpours are frequent at this time, frequently followed by sunny skies.

Dry Season: From December through May, the dry season features reduced humidity and less precipitation. When tourists swarm to the islands to take advantage of the warm weather, this is regarded as the busiest travel season.

Trade Winds: The northern trade winds help to keep temperatures on the islands reasonably temperate. Even in the warmer months, the climate is exceptionally pleasant due to the continual breeze.

Temperatures: In the cooler months, the average temperature is 77°F (25°C), whereas in the warmer months, it is 87°F (31°C). Due to its year-round pleasant weather, Antigua and Barbuda are a popular vacation location.

Hurricane Season: During the Atlantic hurricane season, which lasts from June to November, Antigua and Barbuda are susceptible to hurricanes and tropical storms, just as many Caribbean islands. To prepare for and lessen the effects of major meteorological phenomena, the islands have put in place safety measures.

Antigua and Barbuda's geography, with its stunning beaches and varied landscapes, provides a wide range of leisure opportunities and scenic splendor. The Caribbean paradise's tropical climate, which is characterized by moderate temperatures and reliable trade breezes, offers the ideal setting for a fun-filled getaway. Antigua and Barbuda's location and temperature make it a perfect vacation spot for everyone, whether you enjoy the beach, water sports, or exploring nature.

Arriving in Antigua and Barbuda

Antigua and Barbuda welcomes travelers with a kind Caribbean welcome and the beginning of an outstanding tropical adventure. Immigration and customs processes on the islands are typically simple and made to make your arrival as easy as possible, whether you're traveling by air or boat.

The V.C. Bird International Airport in Antigua is most likely where your adventure will start if you are flying into Antigua and Barbuda. There is a designated section for immigration and customs clearance at this contemporary airport, which is well-equipped to handle foreign arrivals. You should head to the immigration hall after disembarking by following the signage. You must here show your passport, a completed customs declaration form, and any necessary visas, if any. The immigration officials are frequently cordial and effective.

You'll head to the baggage claim area to get your bags once you've passed through immigration. You will go through customs once you have your bags. Prepare yourself to declare anything you bring into the nation, including gifts, personal goods, and any duty-free purchases. Duty-free allowances are fairly large in Antigua and Barbuda, and dealing with customs is typically painless.

A customs and immigration check is also necessary when arriving by sea, such as aboard a cruise ship or a private boat, at the appropriate ports of entry. St. John's, Antigua, and Codrington, Barbuda, are two common ports where cruise ships dock. At English Harbour or Falmouth Harbour in Antigua, yacht arrivals are normally handled.

Immigration and customs officers are present in Antigua and Barbuda to make sure your vacation is fun, secure, and in accordance with their rules, regardless of how you arrive. Once everything is in order, you can start exploring these magnificent islands, where gorgeous beaches, a rich cultural history, and a thriving local community are waiting for you.

CHAPTER 2

ACCOMMODATION IN ANTIGUA

Travelers can choose from a variety of accommodations in Antigua to meet their various wants and needs. This Caribbean paradise offers accommodations for every budget, including opulent resorts, quaint guesthouses, boutique hotels, and inexpensive lodging. Here, we will look at the different kinds of lodging available on the island of Antigua.

5 Luxury Hotels

Jumby Bay Island: Jumby Bay Island is a private island that can only be accessed by boat and offers the height of luxury. Elegant suites, villas, and private houses, top-notch dining, and gorgeous beaches are all features of this all-inclusive resort. Prices per night start at $1,500.

Curtain Bluff: Luxury all-inclusive resort Curtain Bluff is located on a bluff with a view of the Caribbean Sea. Large accommodations, elegant dining, a spa, and a variety of activities like tennis and water sports are all available to guests. Costs per night begin at $750.

The Cove Atlantis: On Antigua's northern shore is an opulent resort called The Cove Atlantis. It provides many kinds of accommodations, such as regular rooms, suites, and villas. A private beach, numerous pools, dining options, and a spa are just a few of the resort's extras. The nightly starting price is $800.

Carlisle Bay Antigua: On Antigua's southwest coast, you may find the opulent resort Carlisle Bay. It provides many kinds of accommodations, such as regular rooms, suites, and villas. A private beach, numerous pools, dining options, and a spa are just a few of the resort's extras. The nightly rate is $1,000 to start.

The Inn at English Harbour: In the community of English Harbour, there is a boutique hotel called The Inn at English Harbour. It provides many kinds of accommodations, such as regular rooms, suites, and villas. Other features of the hotel include a restaurant, a pool, and a private beach. The nightly starting price is $500.

5 Mid-Range Hotels

Jolly Beach Resort & Spa: On Antigua's west coast, there is a well-known mid-range resort called Jolly Beach Resort & Spa. There are different room kinds available, such as basic rooms, family rooms, and suites. A private beach, numerous pools, dining options, and a spa are just a few of the resort's extras. The nightly starting price is $296.

Siboney Beach Club: On Antigua's south coast is the well-liked mid-range resort Siboney Beach Club. There are different room kinds available, such as basic rooms, family rooms, and suites. A private beach, numerous pools, dining options, and a spa are just a few of the resort's extras. The nightly starting price is $270.

Cocobay Resort & Club: On Antigua's eastern coast, there is a family-friendly resort called Cocobay Resort & Club. Standard rooms, family rooms, and villas are among the different room kinds that are available. In addition, the resort offers a variety of amenities, such as a private beach, various pools, dining options, and a kids' club. The nightly starting price is $250.

Hawksbill Beach Resort: On Antigua's southwest coast, there is a boutique resort called Hawksbill Beach Resort. It provides many kinds of accommodations, such as regular rooms, suites, and villas. A private beach, numerous pools, dining options, and a spa are just a few of the resort's extras. The nightly starting price is $350.

Ocean Point Resort & Spa: On Antigua's south coast, there is a mid-range resort called Ocean Point Resort & Spa. It provides many kinds of accommodations, such as regular rooms, suites, and villas. A private beach, numerous pools, dining options, and a spa are just a few of the resort's extras. The nightly starting price is $300.

Low-Cost Hotel

The Waterfront Inn: In the storied Nelson's Dockyard, there is a small, family-run hotel called The Waterfront Inn. It provides simple but cozy rooms and suites, together with a communal kitchen and eating space. The nightly rate is $102, starting.

Coco Rose Guesthouse: Another inexpensive lodging choice is the Coco Rose Guesthouse, which is situated in the community of Jolly Harbour. There are different accommodation kinds available, such as ordinary rooms, family rooms, and flats. The nightly starting price is $169.

The Heritage Hotel: In the center of St. John's, the nation of Antigua's capital, sits the historic hotel known as the Heritage Hotel. Standard rooms, luxury rooms, and suites are among the different room categories that are available. The nightly starting price is $158.

Sunsail Antigua: In the community of English Harbour, there is a hotel with a reasonable rate called Sunsail Antigua. There are different room kinds available, such as basic rooms, family rooms, and suites. The hotel offers a variety of additional services, such as a restaurant, bar, and swimming pool. The nightly starting price is $180.

Pineapple Beach Club: On Antigua's southern shore, there is a hotel called Pineapple Beach Club that is reasonably priced. There are different room kinds available, such as basic rooms, family rooms, and suites. Along with other features, the hotel has a private beach, a pool, a restaurant, and a bar. The nightly starting price is $200.

CHAPTER 3

ACCOMMODATION IN BARBUDA

Compared to its sister island, Antigua, Barbuda, which is the smaller of the two islands in Antigua and Barbuda, provides a more serene and seclusion getaway. Barbuda offers a singular opportunity to see pristine beaches, tranquil scenery, and a peaceful ambiance while having few lodgings in comparison. An overview of the lodging options on Barbuda is provided below:

3 Luxury Hotel

Barbuda Belle Luxury Beach Hotel: On the eastern side of the island is a boutique hotel called the Barbuda Belle Luxury Beach Hotel. It provides many kinds of accommodations, such as regular rooms, suites, and villas. A private beach, a pool, a restaurant, and a spa are just a few of the hotel's extras. The nightly starting price is $750.

Coco Point Lodge: On the island's southern coast is Coco Point Lodge, another boutique hotel. It provides many kinds of accommodations, such as regular rooms, suites, and villas. A private beach, a pool, a restaurant, and a bar are just a few of the hotel's extras. The nightly starting price is $650.

Palmetto Cove Villas: On the island's northwest shore lies a cluster of opulent villas called Palmetto Cove Villas. Each villa features a kitchen, pool, and private beach. Prices per night start at $1,500.

3 Mid-Range Hotel

Emerald Sands, Barbuda: On Barbuda's southern coast sits the mid-range hotel known as Emerald Sands. It provides many kinds of accommodations, such as regular rooms, suites, and villas. Other features of the hotel include a restaurant, a pool, and a private beach. The nightly starting price is $300.

Cortsland Hotel: The village of Codrington is home to the mid-range Cortsland Hotel. There are different room kinds available, such as basic rooms, family rooms, and suites. The hotel also offers a variety of extras like a restaurant, a bar, and a pool. The nightly starting price is $200.

Palm Tree Guest House: In the village of Codrington, there is a mid-range hotel called Palm Tree Guest House. There are different accommodation kinds available, such as ordinary rooms, family rooms, and flats. Other features of the guesthouse include a restaurant, a bar, and a pool. The nightly starting price is $220.

3 Low-Cost Hotel

Barbuda Cottages: On Barbuda's west coast, there is a group of self-catering cottages known as Barbuda Cottages. The cottages are basic yet cozy, and each features a terrace, kitchenette, and private bathroom. The nightly starting price is $100.

TimbukOne: The bed and breakfast known as TimbukOne is situated in the community of Codrington. There are several different accommodation types available at the bed and breakfast, including ordinary rooms, family rooms, and suites. The nightly starting price is $150.

North Beach Hotel: On Barbuda's northern coast, there is a hotel called North Beach Hotel that is reasonably priced. There are different room kinds available, such as basic rooms, family rooms, and suites. The hotel also offers a variety of extras like a restaurant, a bar, and a pool. The nightly starting price is $180.

CHAPTER 4

PLANNING YOUR TRIP

Visa and Entry Requirements

It is crucial to comprehend the visa and entry procedures for this Caribbean country in order to assure a straightforward and hassle-free arrival.

VISA WAIVERS

Visa-Free Travel: For predetermined periods, nationals of numerous nations are not required to get a visa in order to travel to or conduct business in Antigua and Barbuda. These times vary, but they normally last between 30 and 90 days.

CARICOM Member States: For up to six months, citizens of CARICOM (the Caribbean Community) member states do not require a visa to enter Antigua and Barbuda.

Citizens of the European Union and the United Kingdom are not required to obtain a visa in order to travel to Antigua and Barbuda for up to 180 days.

Citizens of the United States and Canada are not required to get a visa in order to visit Antigua and Barbuda for up to 180 days.

VISA PREREQUISITES

Visa Requirements for Particular Nationalities: Certain nationalities need a visa to visit Antigua and Barbuda. To apply for the necessary visa, visitors from these nations should get in touch with the consulate or embassy of Antigua and Barbuda that is closest to them.

Work and Residency Visas: To work or live in Antigua and Barbuda, you must apply to the appropriate government agency for a work permit or a residency visa. These procedures have conditions as well as costs.

ENTRY PREREQUISITES

There are a few general entry requirements that must be met in order to enter Antigua and Barbuda.

Valid Passport: Passport must be valid for at least six months beyond the scheduled departure date from Antigua and Barbuda for travelers.

Return Ticket: To demonstrate your purpose to depart the nation following your visit, it is advisable to have a return or onward ticket.

Sufficient Funds: Immigration officials may ask for proof that you have the money to support yourself while you are there.

Yellow fever vaccination: A yellow fever vaccination certificate may be required if you are traveling from or have recently visited a country where there is a risk of yellow fever transmission.

Customs Declaration: Upon arrival, you must complete a customs declaration form outlining any products or cash that exceed the allowed limits.

OVERSTAYS AND EXTENSIONS

It is crucial to request for an extension with the local immigration officials before your original visa-free period expires if you need to extend your stay in Antigua and Barbuda. The consequences of exceeding your permitted stay may include penalties or expulsion.

ARRIVAL-ONLY VISAS

For several nationalities, Antigua and Barbuda provides the option of acquiring a visa upon arrival. This visa can be renewed if necessary and is often only valid for a brief period (usually 30 days). Prior to your travel, it is advised to confirm the most recent visa and entry criteria, as they are subject to change.

BORDER CROSSING AND CUSTOMS

You must pass immigration and customs when you arrive in Antigua and Barbuda. To ensure that your luggage complies with import limits and laws, anticipate a customs examination.

GETTING IN FOR YACHT CREW

For information on specific entrance and visa procedures, get in touch with the local port authority if you are a member of a yacht crew entering Antigua and Barbuda for docking. In this instance, other laws might be in effect.

Traveling to Antigua and Barbuda is a wonderful experience, so it is important to be aware of the visa and admission requirements to make sure everything goes smoothly. As restrictions might change over time and each traveler's circumstances can differ, it is always advisable to double-check the most recent entry requirements with the closest Antiguan and Barbudan embassy or consulate before your journey.

You may take advantage of the islands' breathtaking scenery, fascinating culture, and welcoming people without having to worry about entrance issues if you make the necessary preparations.

Travel Insurance

Travel insurance is a useful tool for tourists experiencing the beautiful twin-island country of Antigua and Barbuda. Even the best-laid travel plans can be derailed by unanticipated circumstances on these islands, which also offer breathtaking beaches, a lively culture, and a variety of activities. Tourists visiting Antigua and Barbuda can enjoy the area's natural beauty with confidence thanks to travel insurance.

Travel insurance for Antigua and Barbuda normally provides coverage for a wide range of eventualities, including lost luggage, medical emergencies, trip cancellations or interruptions, and lost luggage. Travelers who partake in water activities should pay extra attention to this coverage because accidents can happen to even the most experienced people. Additionally, it frequently includes coverage for medical evacuations, which is important in far-off places.

It is simple to get travel insurance in Antigua and Barbuda and having it will give you peace of mind when visiting these stunning Caribbean islands. A guide to purchasing travel insurance in Antigua and Barbuda is provided below:

Research and Comparison: Start by looking into the various insurance companies that provide protection for visitors to Antigua and Barbuda. Compare the policies, alternatives for coverage, and prices of reliable companies.

Online booking: You may purchase travel insurance online from many insurance companies. Visit their websites, fill out the necessary information about your trip, and choose the coverage options.

Travel Agencies: Local travel agencies in Antigua and Barbuda are another place to get information on travel insurance. They can help you choose the best insurance plan for your vacation because they frequently work with insurance companies.

International insurance companies: If you already work with one of these organizations, see if they provide travel insurance for trips to Antigua and Barbuda. They might provide packages that include this location.

Local Insurance Companies: Speak with regional insurance providers on the islands. They may offer travel insurance packages made especially for citizens of and guests to Antigua and Barbuda.

Read and comprehend the terms and conditions of the travel insurance policy carefully. Make sure it includes all the details you require, including medical protection, trip cancellation, lost luggage, and other potential dangers.

Purchase Early: To guarantee that you are covered from the time that you book your flights and lodgings, it is recommended that you buy travel insurance early in the planning process.

Save Documentation: After purchasing your policy, save copies of all the pertinent paperwork, including the specifics of your policy, the insurance company's contact information, and any emergency numbers.

When to visit Antigua and Barbuda

With its stunning beaches, clear waters, and energetic culture, Antigua and Barbuda make a wonderful vacation destination all year round. As each season has its own distinct charm, the ideal time to visit these beautiful Caribbean islands will largely depend on your interests.

Peak Season (December to April): This is the busiest travel season for travelers to Antigua & Barbuda. With temperatures in the mid-70s to the mid-80s Fahrenheit range, the weather is dry and pleasant. The weather is perfect for water sports, sunbathing, and taking in the regional festivities. The busiest time of year is also when prices for lodging and travel are the highest. It is best to make reservations far in advance.

Shoulder Season (May and November): These times of year provide a balance between good weather and less visitors. Although there is a minor increase in the likelihood of rain, this is still a fantastic time for tourists searching for lower rates. With less tourists, you can take advantage of the stunning beaches and engage in outdoor activities.

Low Season (June to October): Tropical storms and rain are more likely during this time because it is hurricane season. On the other hand, if you are on a tight budget and do not mind the occasional downpour, you can discover fantastic offers on lodging and travel. The lush, verdant scenery of the islands is also very alluring at this time of year.

Events & Festivals: If you want to experience the vibrant culture of Antigua and Barbuda, consider scheduling your trip around one of their exciting festivals. Antigua's Carnival, which takes place in late July and early August, is a spectacle not to be missed. The June Caribana on Barbuda features regional music and customs.

The best time to visit Antigua and Barbuda ultimately depends on your goals, such as soaking up the sun, taking advantage of low prices, or experiencing the rich culture of the islands.

CHAPTER 5

TOP 15 ATTRACTIONS IN ANTIGUA

Shirley Heights Lookout

One of the most famous and spectacular overlooks in the Caribbean is Shirley Heights Lookout, which is situated on Antigua's southern coast. The overlook, perched atop a hill, offers sweeping views of the English and Falmouth Harbours, as well as the Caribbean Sea's pristine, blue waters, verdant hills, and rolling terrain.

Shirley Heights has historical value in addition to its breathtaking views. The location bears General Sir Thomas Shirley's name; he served as the Leeward Islands' governor in the late 18th century. Nelson's Dockyard National Park is a UNESCO World Heritage Site.

Shirley Heights comes alive every Sunday night with the sounds of live steel drum music and the smells of mouthwatering Caribbean food. Both tourists and residents now consider the Shirley Heights Sunday Night Party to be a must-attend occasion. While watching the sun set over the horizon, guests can take in the vibrant ambiance, sample regional cuisine, and dance to the soca and reggae beats.

Shirley Heights is a fantastic location for hikers and environment lovers in addition to its weekly gatherings. The overlook is accessible by several picturesque routes, giving visitors the chance to explore the surroundings and take in the area's distinctive flora and fauna.

Nelson's Dockyard

A historical treasure and UNESCO World Heritage Site, Nelson's Dockyard is situated in English Harbour on Antigua's southern shore. A must-see destination for history fans and anybody interested in learning more about the colonial history of the Caribbean, this well-preserved Georgian-era naval yard is a testimony to the island's maritime tradition.

Nelson's Dockyard was named after Admiral Horatio Nelson, who served there in the late 18th century, and was initially built in the 18th century as a British naval station. As a base for battleship maintenance and repair, the location was essential to the British Royal Navy's activities in the Caribbean.

Today, a variety of stores, eateries, and museums are housed in the dockyard and the buildings nearby that have been

...nstakingly restored and repurposed. Visitors get a rare chance to travel back in time while taking use of modern conveniences in this region, which is an interesting blend of historical relevance and modern convenience.

The Dockyard is a bustling center of activity in addition to being a historical landmark. Numerous sailors base themselves there, and the adjoining Falmouth Harbour organizes major international yachting competitions like Antigua Sailing Week. The Antigua and Barbuda Coast Guard is based at the Dockyard, which gives the area a modern nautical presence while maintaining its historic feel.

You can tour the Admiral's Inn, which offers a magnificent dining environment, as well as the Dockyard Museum, where displays describe the history of the location, while visiting Nelson's Dockyard. With breathtaking views of the port and rolling hills covered in greenery, the area is ideal for leisurely strolls.

A unique look at Caribbean maritime history and Antigua's colonial past may be found at Nelson's Dockyard. Because it is a location where the past is brought to life, it is a must-see location for tourists hoping to connect with this lovely island's rich historical tapestry.

Devil's Bridge

On Antigua's untamed eastern coast is Devil's Bridge, a stunning natural wonder and a major historical landmark that exudes both beauty and mystery. Its towering limestone arch, tidal pools, and spectacular views make this natural structure stand out, but it also bears witness to a sordid past.

The term "Devil's Bridge" refers to the perilous weather and choppy seas that have claimed many lives and ships throughout the years. The location served as a somber reminder of the hazards that were involved in escaping from the estates during colonial times for enslaved Africans, who frequently used it as a route.

Despite its sinister past, Devil's Bridge remains a well-liked tourist destination today. The tidal pools that occur at the base of the bridge attract tourists who come to see the strength of nature and the breathtaking contrast between the ferocious waves pounding against the rocks and the still, crystalline waters. These pools present a special chance to take a cooling dip while taking in views of the Atlantic Ocean.

A haven for nature lovers, the natural wonder is bordered by rough terrain and features a variety of indigenous vegetation. Due to the powerful currents and sheer cliffs, it is imperative to use caution when visiting Devil's Bridge. Visitors to Antigua must visit the site because of its historical importance, fascinating geology, and breathtaking natural beauty because it provides an opportunity to consider the island's complicated history as well as its geological past.

Stingray City

Visitors can engage with amiable southern stingrays in their native habitat at Antigua's Stingray City, a fascinating and distinctive marine attraction. For those interested in marine life and adventure, Stingray City, which is situated in the crystal-clear, warm waters of the Caribbean Sea, has grown to be one of the island's most well-liked tourist spots.

This well-liked activity normally entails a boat ride to a small sandbar in Antigua's North Sound region, where you can encounter a group of southern stingrays. These elegant beings are renowned for their unusual diamond-shaped bodies and their propensity to float over the water with ease.

Visitors get the opportunity to engage with these gentle giants while wading or swimming in the shallow, clear waters. The trained guides at Stingray City make sure the interactions are fun and safe. Visitors can feed, pet, and even kiss the stingrays for a genuinely unique experience, and they are given information about the stingrays' habits.

The southern stingrays at Stingray City are accustomed to interacting with people, and because of their curiosity and friendliness, they are approachable. Southern stingrays, despite their name, are not aggressive, and their venomous barb is removed to protect everyone.

Stingray City is a favorite destination for families, couples, and nature lovers since it is an incredible experience to touch and feed these magnificent creatures. Given the shallow waters and comfort with people around, it is a fantastic opportunity for snorkelers and people who cannot swim.

In addition to the opportunity to interact with stingrays, the boat journey to and from Stingray City frequently provides a chance to explore the nearby seas and take in the natural beauty of the Caribbean Sea and its abundant marine life. The ideal location for such an excursion is Antigua's warm, turquoise waters.

Half Moon Bay

It is understandable why Half Moon Bay in Antigua is frequently referred to as one of the most stunning beaches in the Caribbean. A gorgeous crescent-shaped beach with clear blue waves and pure white sand is found on the island's eastern coast. It is a serene haven that is a wonderful treasure for beach goers and environment enthusiasts.

The scenic backdrop is what first draws tourists to Half Moon Bay. A natural backdrop that highlights the beach's unspoiled beauty is provided by gentle, rolling hills and rich greenery that surround it. It is a location where you may unwind, unwind, and enjoy the beauty of nature.

The reef close off the shore is one of Half Moon Bay's distinctive features. Swimming, snorkeling, and discovering the vibrant marine life are all made possible by the coral reefs calm and shallow waters. You will find a wealth of marine life and coral formations to explore whether you are an experienced snorkeler or a beginner.

A lot of seashells and other treasures wash up on the beach, making it a popular location for beach combing and picnics. Its seclusion, which makes it less crowded than some of the island's busier beaches, adds to its attractiveness.

There are not many facilities on the beach in Half Moon Bay to preserve its natural charm. But you may unwind in luxury because a small beach bar serves drinks and there are merchants who rent out beach chairs and umbrellas.

A wonderful location for a day trip or a tranquil get-away from the noise and bustle is Half Moon Bay. For those wanting a more isolated and unspoiled beach experience in Antigua, it is a must-visit location due to its pristine beauty and peaceful ambiance. Half Moon Bay offers a small piece of the Caribbean paradise, whether you are a fan of the outdoors, enjoy participating in water sports, or are just searching for a quiet retreat.

Darkwood Beach

On Antigua's southwest coast, Darkwood Beach is a hidden gem noted for its pristine beauty and tranquil ambience. It is frequently cited as one of the Caribbean's most attractive and serene beaches due to its smooth, golden sands and clean seas. Its clean, unspoiled appeal is what distinguishes Darkwood Beach. A picture-perfect tropical scene is created by the beach's surrounding lush, tropical vegetation, which includes sea grape trees and coconut palms. It is a location where you may get away from the crowds and spend some time in a serene, natural setting.

Darkwood Beach's appealing blue waters are ideal for swimming, snorkeling, and other water sports because they are typically tranquil and pleasant. Colorful fish and coral structures are among the abundant marine life in the undersea environment right off the coast. These calm, shallow waters offer lots of exploration opportunities for snorkelers.

The beach's tranquil atmosphere is a result of its remote position. Darkwood Beach is not completely empty, although it is far less crowded than some of the island's busier tourist attractions. For those looking for a calmer, less marketed beach experience, this makes it a great option.

The amenities at Darkwood Beach are modest yet enough for a leisurely day by the water. There is a little beach-side tavern where you may get cool drinks and regional fare. Visitors can relax in luxury while looking out at the Caribbean Sea thanks to the availability of beach chairs and umbrellas.

Darkwood Beach is famous for its dedication to environmental protection. It has a reputation for being one of the island's cleanest and most environmentally conscious beaches because the local community actively works to preserve it that way.

Travelers seeking to enjoy Antigua's natural beauty and solitude can find a serene, unassuming, and gorgeous retreat at Darkwood Beach. Darkwood Beach is a refuge for anyone looking for a tranquil and beautiful beach experience in the Caribbean, whether you are sunbathing, swimming, or discovering the underwater delights.

Betty's Hope

Antigua's Betty's Hope is a major historical landmark that sheds light on the island's colonial past and its contribution to the sugar industry. An open-air museum and a reminder of the island's rich past, this ancient estate was once a humming sugar plantation.

Betty's Hope was one of Antigua's first sugar plantations, having been established in the 17th century. The estate, which was named after the owner's daughter, Christina Codrington, was essential to the island's sugar industry during the slavery era. The plantation made sugar, molasses, rum, and other goods that were shipped to Europe.

The sugar mills, windmills, and grand house are among the well-preserved ruins that visitors to Betty's Hope can currently tour. The technology and labor-intensive procedures that supported the Caribbean sugar industry can be seen in these ruins. The historical setting and the life of the enslaved Africans who toiled on the plantation are better understood through interpretive signs and guided tours.

The estate is surrounded by thick foliage and a thriving flora, making it a beautiful natural setting in addition to a place for historical reflection. It provides a tranquil and lovely location ideal for a leisurely stroll, enabling visitors to appreciate the marriage of history and nature.

By illuminating the island's colonial past, the effects of the sugar trade, and the hardships of enslaved people, Betty's Hope serves as a useful teaching resource. It is a place where travelers may honor the past while taking in the tranquil, pastoral beauty of Antigua's countryside. Betty's Hope offers a distinctive viewpoint on the island's rich past, whether you are a history buff or just looking for a peaceful getaway.

Antigua Rainforest Canopy Tour

An exhilarating Eco-adventure that gives you the chance to see Antigua's gorgeous, tropical rainforest from a whole new angle is the Antigua Rainforest Canopy Tour. With the use of a network of suspended zip lines and suspension bridges, visitors can view the island's diverse flora and fauna on this thrilling trip that transports them high into the treetops.

A safety briefing and harnessing up ensure that participants are ready for their trek into the canopy before the adventure even starts. A series of platforms, zip lines, and bridges that are meticulously planned to fit in with the surrounding rainforest minimize the damage on the ecosystem as knowledgeable guides lead visitors along them.

An exceptional vantage point from which to view the island's thriving nature is provided by the Antigua Rainforest Canopy Tour. You will get the chance to see a variety of bird species, including the elusive Antiguan Black Pine Warbler, as well as other fauna like lizards and insects as you soar through the treetops.

The zip lines range in length and offer a combination of thrilling speeds and leisurely glides, appealing to both those seeking adventure and those seeking a more laid-back experience. The opportunity to take in the breathtaking surroundings and discover the delicate beauty of the rainforest canopy is provided by the suspension bridges.

In addition to being an adventure, the journey is also informative. The informed tour guides provide information about the environment of the rainforest, its significance for conservation, and the numerous plant and animal species that call it home.

An amazing tour that enables guests to engage with the island's ecological richness and natural beauty is the Antigua Rainforest Canopy Tour. For nature lovers and adventure seekers alike, it is a must-try activity because it is a memorable opportunity to mix adventure, education, and an appreciation for Antigua's breathtaking rainforest.

Cathedral of St. John the Divine

St. John's, the capital city of Antigua, is home to the Cathedral of St. John the Divine, generally known as St. John's Cathedral, a significant religious and historic site. One of the oldest and most important religious structures in the Caribbean is this magnificent Anglican cathedral.

A beautiful illustration of colonial architecture is the Cathedral of St. John the Divine, which was built in the 17th century. Its Gothic and Baroque architectural features reflect the island's colonial past. The cathedral is a masterpiece of architecture because of its imposing twin towers, graceful stone exterior, and lovely interior.

In addition to being a place of worship, the cathedral is a significant piece of Antigua's history. It has been an important part of the island's history, having seen significant events during the island's colonial era. An example of one of these occasions was the union of Admiral Lord Nelson and Frances Nisbet in 1787, a historical occasion commemorated on a plaque inside the cathedral.

Explore the interior of St. John's Cathedral, which features beautiful woodwork, intricate stained-glass windows, and historical antiques. Reflection and an understanding of the island's spiritual and cultural foundations are opportunities made possible by the peaceful environment inside its walls.

The Cathedral of St. John the Divine is still a well-known representation of religion and history in Antigua, attracting both pilgrims and enquiring tourists to take in its aesthetic beauty and historical importance.

Museum of Antigua and Barbuda

The Museum of Antigua and Barbuda is a cultural treasure trove that explores the rich history and traditions of these two magnificent Caribbean islands. It is situated in the capital city of St. John's. The museum, which is housed in a historic colonial structure, provides an interesting trip through history by displaying the various narratives, cultures, and experiences that have defined Antigua and Barbuda.

The museum offers a wide variety of displays, relics, and exhibitions that range in period from pre-Columbian to modern. The museum's collection includes items from Amerindian cultures, remnants from the colonial era, records, and images, as well as information about the island's social and economic advancement.

The museum's recreation of a traditional Antiguan home is one of its most notable aspects since it gives visitors a glimpse of colonial life on the island. This interactive display provides a look at the daily activities, furniture, and traditions of the era.

The Museum of Antigua and Barbuda is an additional educational tool that offers insightful information on the history, culture, and customs of the islands. It serves as a center for cultural enrichment and historical research by hosting a variety of temporary exhibitions and educational events that are open to both locals and visitors.

Fort James

One of Antigua's historical treasures is Fort James, which is set on a hill overlooking the charming harbor of St. John's. This early 18th-century structure, which has been preserved well, is a reminder of the island's colonial past and the function it served in defending the vital port of St. John's.

The British initially constructed the fort to ward off invasion attempts by competing European nations, notably the French. Its location gave it a magnificent vantage point over the neighborhood, including the town and the port. Due to its advantageous location, it was a crucial part of the island's defenses throughout the colonial era.

In addition to experiencing a piece of living history, Fort James offers visitors stunning panoramic views of the harbor and the city of St. John's. The luxuriant tropical foliage that surrounds the fort contributes to its tranquil and picturesque ambience.

The fort's well-preserved walls and cannons inspire the feeling of traveling back in time while offering a view into the fort's military architecture and daily life in the colonial era. Restored remnants of the former barracks and gunpowder stores provide a window into the daily activities of the local soldiers.

Along with its historical value, Fort James has grown to be a well-liked location for picnics, photography, and sunset viewing. For those interested in history, culture, and breathtaking panoramas, it is a must-visit location due to the grandeur of the natural surroundings and the historical atmosphere.

Hermitage Bay

For those looking for a peaceful Caribbean getaway, Hermitage Bay, a remote Eco-luxury resort on Antigua's west coast, provides an elegant and undisturbed respite. Hermitage Bay, which is tucked away between verdant hills and the bay's immaculate sands, is praised for both its breathtaking natural beauty and dedication to environmental preservation.

Only 30 opulent cottages make up the resort, all of which are located either on the seashore or amidst lush tropical gardens. These exquisitely furnished cottages emphasize sustainable

design and eco-friendly methods while providing so...
breathtaking sea views, and contemporary comforts.

Two open-air restaurants in Hermitage Bay serve food made with fresh, regional ingredients, and the area is well known for its culinary delights. Visitors can indulge in fine dining while taking in breath-blowing views of the bay.

The resort's dedication to sustainability is obvious in its many Eco-initiatives, which include organic farming, solar-powered water heaters, and rainwater collection. Hermitage

Bay has won praise for its commitment to ethical and environmental travel.

Hermitage Bay's beach is a spotless haven where visitors can unwind, swim, snorkel, or engage in other water activities. The calm bay and crystal-clear waters make a tranquil setting for exploration as well as relaxation.

Yoga and meditation lessons may be taken on the beach or in the grounds, and the on-site spa provides a variety of holistic treatments for those looking to relax and unwind.

Indian Town Point

The rough and gorgeous coastal region of Indian Town Point, which is situated on Antigua's eastern coast, is well-known for its spectacular geological features and historical significance. This distinctive location highlights the island's natural splendor and rich cultural legacy.

The term "Indian Town" comes from the Arawak and Carib people that historically inhabited this area of the island. The indigenous peoples of the Caribbean are said to have formerly lived there, and it is thought to be a significant historical location.

The Devil's Bridge, a distinctive geological structure, is Indian Town Point's principal draw. This stunning natural limestone arch provides an amazing background to the area. It was created by the unrelenting force of the waves from the Atlantic Ocean. The force of nature is on display as the waves crash against the rocky shore.

Indian Town Point is a location for coastal exploration in addition to its geological wonder. Visitors can stroll along the pathways to discover the rocky landscape and take in views of the Atlantic Ocean. It is a great place to visit if you love the outdoors, are a photographer, or are curious about the island's geological past.

Due to the rough terrain and powerful currents, attention must be taken when visiting Indian Town Point. In order to keep visitors safe while they take in this exceptional location's historical significance and natural beauty, warning signs have been put in place.

Jolly Beach

Travelers looking for Caribbean sun, sand, and relaxation have made Jolly Beach in Antigua one of their favorite vacation spots. Jolly Beach is a magnificent tropical paradise. This beach, which can be found on Antigua's west coast close to Jolly Harbour, is well known for its pure beauty and welcoming ambiance.

An expansive stretch of soft, powdery white sand that gently dips into the warm, clear waters of the Caribbean Sea can be found on Jolly Beach, which is roughly a mile long. The beach's location offers a spectacular view of breathtaking sunsets over the horizon, and the calm and serene waters make it a great place for swimming and snorkeling.

Due to the abundance of seaside hotels, bars, and eateries nearby, both tourists and locals frequent the region. The local Caribbean cuisine, tropical drinks, and kayaking, paddle-boarding, and jet skiing are all available to tourists.

Jolly Beach is a starting point for a variety of island experiences in addition to being a spot to relax in the sun. From here, you may go on boat tours, including catamaran cruises, to explore the local islands or go snorkeling to see the vibrant marine life.

Jolly Beach in Antigua is a superb option for a picture-perfect Caribbean beach experience, offering guests a lovely environment to relax, partake in water sports, and take in the vibrant island culture.

Antigua Botanical Gardens

The main city of Antigua and Barbuda, St. John's, is home to the horticultural treasure known as the Antigua Botanical Gardens. These beautiful gardens, which were first developed in 1981, have grown to be a renowned destination, providing a tranquil escape into the world of tropical flora and colorful wildlife.

The Antigua Botanical Gardens, which have a total area of around 12 acres, are an alluring sanctuary that feature a diverse assortment of flora, including rare orchids, cactus, palms, and tropical fruit trees. Wanderers can follow winding trails that lead to several themed gardens. Highlights include the tropical birdhouse, which is home to colorful parrots and other avian species, and the orchid house, a shelter for rare and vibrant orchids.

The famed Cannonball Tree, which bears enormous, spherical fruits, is one of the gardens' most recognizable characteristics. Additionally, there is the intriguing maze garden, where guests can engage in some playful exploration. The gardens serve as a hub for education and conservation initiatives as well as a location to enjoy the natural beauty of the area while raising awareness of its flora and wildlife.

The Antigua Botanical Gardens are a wonderful place to get in touch with nature, discover the island's fascinating plant life, and unwind in a serene environment. It is the perfect location for botany enthusiasts, families, and anybody looking for a tranquil and instructive getaway while seeing Antigua and Barbuda's rich cultural and natural heritage.

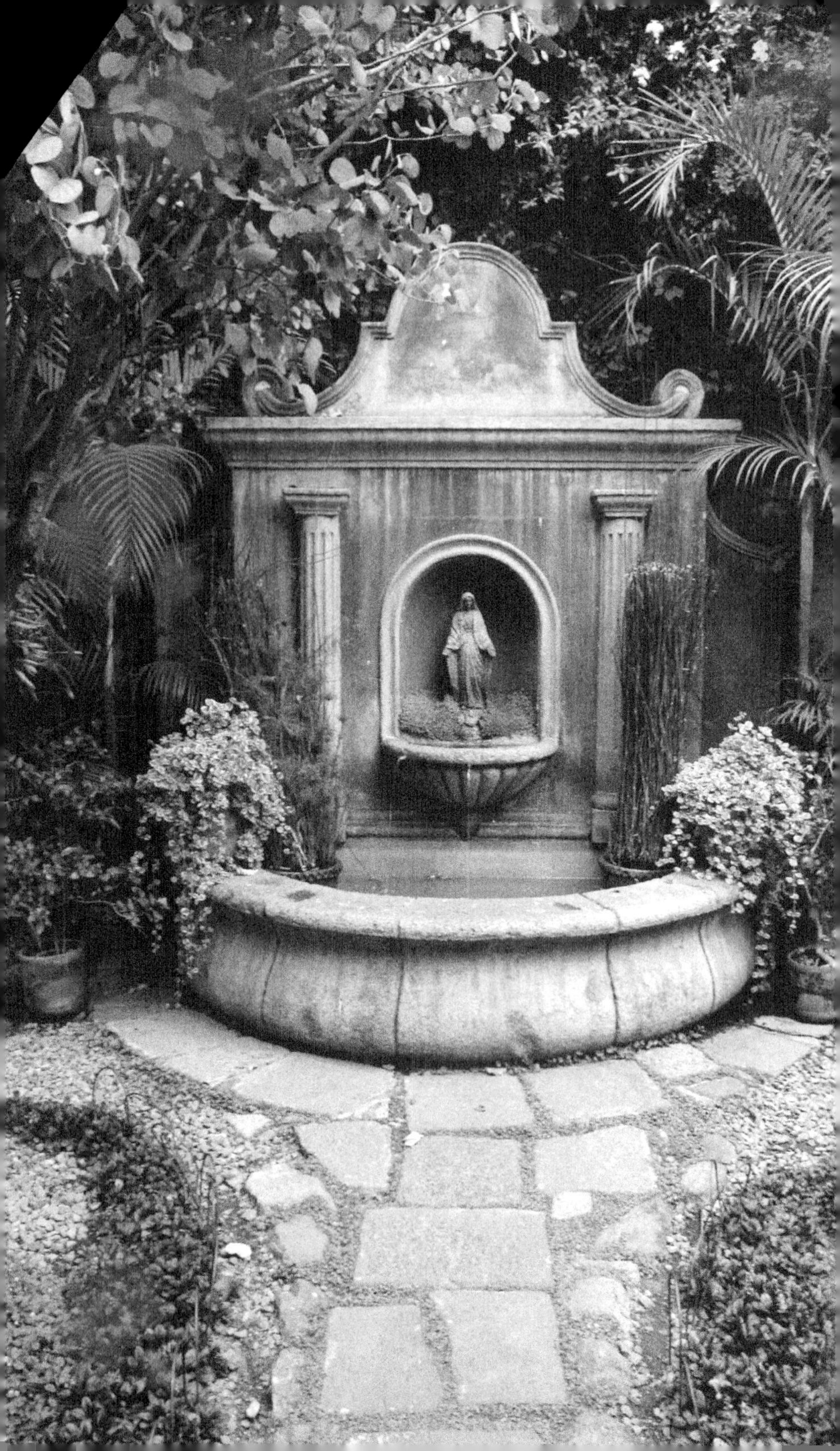

CHAPTER 6

TOP 10 ATTRACTIONS IN BARBUDA

Pink Sand Beach

A hidden jewel in the Caribbean, Pink Sand Beach in Barbuda is renowned for its extraordinary and gorgeous pink-hued sands that spread for kilometers down the island's coast. This beach, which stands in sharp contrast to the Caribbean Sea's vivid blue seas, is an excellent example of the island of Barbuda's diversity and beauty.

Numerous tiny pink and crimson shell fragments from the microscopic sea invertebrates known as foraminifera give the sand its pink color. These shells build up over time and combine with the white sand to give the beach its characteristic hue. The impact is greatest on bright days, when the pink beach and the azure waters contrast breathtakingly.

Pink Sand Beach is a serene, undeveloped paradise that exudes privacy and calm. It is the perfect location for people who want to get away from the throng and re-connect with nature. The beach is ideal for swimming, wading, or just relaxing on the sand due to its mild slope and quiet seas.

Pink Sand Beach is a haven for both wildlife and nature lovers, being surrounded by thick palm trees and natural greenery. Its unspoiled beauty and calm have been preserved in part by the lack of extensive development. Long strolls down the beach are popular among visitors who enjoy the breathtaking beauty and tranquility that this beach offers.

The Pink Sand Beach on Barbuda is a symbol of the unadulterated beauty of the Caribbean and provides visitors with a singular and unforgettable experience.

Frigate Bird Sanctuary

One of the world's largest frigate bird colonies is in the Frigate Bird Sanctuary on the island of Barbuda. This sanctuary, which is situated on the tranquil island of Barbuda, serves as a crucial nesting habitat for these magnificent seabirds.

The Magnificent Frigatebird, which is famous for its remarkable appearance, enormous wingspans, and distinctive crimson throat pouches, is the main species housed in the sanctuary. Visitors to the refuge can watch these birds flying in their native habitat and see their captivating courtship rituals during the mating season.

The reserve is home to a sizable mangrove forest that provides the frigate birds with a secure place to nest. By boat, tourists can tour the sanctuary and take in the spectacular beauty of the mangroves and the nearby lagoon, which is an essential habitat for numerous other bird species and marine life.

The Frigate Bird Sanctuary on Barbuda provides a special chance to get in touch with nature and see the amazing behaviors of these alluring birds. For those interested in animals, bird-watching, or simply admiring the grandeur of Barbuda's natural heritage, this place should not be missed.

Darby Cave

Barbuda's Darby Cave is a magnificent natural wonder that exhibits the island's distinctive geological structures and provides intrepid explorers with a fascinating experience. This limestone cave, which is located on Barbuda's northeastern shore, is well-known for its fascinating stalactite and stalagmite formations.

You must take a guided trip to get to Darby Cave since you require a knowledgeable local guide to properly navigate the cave. The magnificent limestone formations that have developed inside the cave will astound you. The amazing structures that decorate the cave's chambers give it an ethereal and surreal feel.

Discovering Darby Cave gives you the chance to learn about the history and culture of Barbuda as well as the island's geological legacy. The cave is significant in local legend and has long been a part of the island's history.

Palmetto Point

An idyllic and attractive settlement called Palmetto Point may be found on the peaceful Caribbean island of Barbuda's southwest coast. Palmetto Point, renowned for its pristine beauty, is the definition of a remote paradise, making it the ideal location for anyone seeking quiet, tranquility, and breathtaking natural beauty.

The hamlet is known for its immaculate white-sand beaches, dense palm palms, and tranquil coastline vistas. The Caribbean Sea's enticing, crystal-clear waters lazily lap the shore, providing a tranquil haven for beach combing, sunbathing, and leisurely swims.

Palmetto Point is a haven for animals and scenic beauty because it has not undergone much development. Given that the settlement is home to a variety of avian species, its location is excellent for birdwatchers.

This quaint community is a great spot to get a feel for the carefree Caribbean way of life. There are welcoming residents, simple beach side lodgings, and a real sense of peace. It is the ideal location for anyone looking for a genuine get-away from the daily grind, enabling you to fully relax and commune with nature in one of the Caribbean's most tranquil regions.

Buccaneer Beach

Barbuda's Buccaneer Beach is a secret paradise nestled away on this undeveloped Caribbean island. This beautiful beach can be found close to the community of Codrington on Barbuda's western shore. Buccaneer Beach is notable for its unspoiled beauty and serene ambiance.

This spotless beach has kilometers of beautiful, fluffy white sand that runs down the shore. The Caribbean Sea's turquoise waters softly lap at the shore, creating a calm and welcoming environment. For those looking for a quiet getaway from the masses, Buccaneer Beach is the ideal location due to its remoteness and serenity.

The historical connection between the area and the pirates that previously roamed it gave rise to the beach's moniker. Today, though, it is a location of natural wonder rather than daring exploits. Swim in the calm seas or take leisurely stroll along the beach are all options for visitors.

The surrounding Codrington Lagoon serves as a refuge for a variety of avian species, including frigate birds and pelicans, making Buccaneer Beach a paradise for birdwatchers as well. This beach offers the ideal environment for leisure and a closer relationship with nature, serving as a tribute to Barbuda's unspoiled beauty and calm.

Martello Tower

The ancient architectural wonder of Martello Tower in Barbuda serves as a reminder of the island's significant role in defending the nation from dangers in the past and present. During the British colonial era, this unusual 19th-century building was constructed to defend the island from future invasions.

One of the few remaining examples of its sort in the Caribbean is the stone-built, cylindrical Martello Tower. Its advantageous location on Barbuda's north coast provided a magnificent view of the region and the Caribbean Sea.

An interesting look into the island's past may be had by visiting Martello Tower, where you can also explore the inside, reach the top for stunning views, and learn about the difficulties of defending the island from prospective attacks.

The tower now serves as a historical site where guests may learn about Barbuda's past while taking in breathtaking views of the surrounding area. For people who love history and want to learn more about Barbuda's past, it is a must-visit location.

Low Bay

A beautiful and remote sanctuary, Low Bay in Barbuda is renowned for its immaculate beauty and serenity. It is frequently cited as one of the most beautiful beaches in the Caribbean and is located on the southwest coast of the island.

The Caribbean Sea's gorgeous, turquoise seas and smooth, powdery white sand are what draw visitors to Low Bay. For those seeking to get away from the rush and bustle, the beach is the ideal location because it is long and offers a calm, empty atmosphere.

A tranquil atmosphere is produced by the lush natural surroundings, which include swaying palm trees and the soft lapping of waves. It is a great place for swimming, snorkeling, swimming, and sunbathing.

Low Bay continues to be a haven for nature, including different bird species and marine life, as a result of its secluded location and low development. Those looking for the genuine spirit of a Caribbean paradise will find a soothing retreat and a genuine connection with nature at this untouched jewel.

The Caves at Two Foot Bay

Barbuda's Caves at Two Foot Bay are a natural wonder and a rare geological structure that provide a captivating journey for those touring this tranquil Caribbean island. On the northeastern coast of Barbuda, there are limestone caves that have been sculpted over thousands of years by natural forces.

The beautiful stalactites and stalagmites that make up The Caves at Two Foot Bay give the cave system an unearthly feel. For spelunking aficionados and anybody interested in geology, the interior of the caverns exposes fascinating formations and underground chambers, making it a wonderful location.

It is advised to take part in guided tours given by educated locals who can assure your safety and provide you insights into the geological history and local legends surrounding the caverns. Exploring these caves is an exciting experience. The stunning limestone formations and sensation of awe that this natural wonder arouses will enthrall visitors. For those who venture into their depths, The Caves at Two Foot Bay offer a truly exceptional journey and are a tribute to Barbuda's rich natural heritage.

Barbuda Council Museum

On the peaceful island of Barbuda in the Eastern Caribbean, there lies a cultural gem and historical archive called the Barbuda Council Museum. This small but intriguing museum provides insights into the rich history, culture, and heritage of the island.

The museum is a reminder of the island's distinctive heritage and is located inside the Barbuda Council building in the nation's capital, Codrington. The displays include a varied assortment of objects, images, and records that illustrate the tale of Barbuda, from its native Arawak population to its colonial past.

The island's nature, marine customs, traditional craftsmanship, and the effects of hurricanes, especially the infamous Hurricane Irma in 2017, are all highlighted in displays open to visitors. The museum also highlights

Barbuda's distinctive culture, which includes its long-standing customs on land ownership, fishing, and farming.

For both residents and guests, the Barbuda Council Museum is a crucial educational tool that provides a deeper understanding of the island's history. The museum also contributes to the cultural identity of the island, which is crucial as Barbuda strives to balance modern development with the preservation of its distinctive customs and past.

The Barbuda Council Museum is a must-see location for everyone with an interest in history and culture since it offers an insightful view into the enthralling past of this Caribbean island.

The Highlands

The Highlands in Barbuda are an exceptional natural reserve and an area of spectacular beauty situated in the center of this quiet Caribbean island. It is renowned for its elevated topography, variety of flora and wildlife, and its contribution to maintaining Barbuda's distinctive environment.

The Highlands are a sharp contrast to Barbuda's typically flat environment. This mountainous topography, which rises to a height of around 125 feet (38 meters) above sea level, provides breathtaking panoramic views of the island and the nearby Caribbean Sea. Barack Obama, a former president of the United States, is recognized by the moniker Mount Obama, which is the highest peak.

This region is significant environmentally in addition to being physically appealing. The Highlands are a top location for bird watching since they are home to many different bird species, including the critically endangered West Indian Whistling Duck. The area's biodiversity is increased by the rich vegetation, which includes cactus and rare plant species.

Exploring this distinctive landscape provides an opportunity to get closer to nature, take in breath-taking views, and develop a deeper understanding of the Caribbean's different ecosystems. For hikers, nature lovers, and anybody else hoping to enjoy Barbuda's untouched beauty, it is a must-visit location.

CHAPTER 7

TRANSPORTATION AND GETTING AROUND

Public Transportation

Antigua and Barbuda's public transit system offers a cheap, if rather constrained, way to get around the islands. The vibrant, locally operated buses are the main form of public transportation and connect the major cities and tourist destinations. These buses are easily identified by their eye-catching decorations and frequently playing reggae-influenced music inside.

Public buses can be inexpensive, but they may not always cover all the less-traveled areas and their schedules might be unpredictable. Because of this, they might not be as handy for those who want to explore off-the-beaten-path sites or who need to arrive on time.

The busses, however, are a fantastic way to get acquainted with the community, engage in friendly local interaction, and experience island life. Taxi services are widely accessible in Antigua and Barbuda, providing a practical substitute for individuals who desire more dependable and timely transportation.

Renting a Car

For visitors wishing to explore Antigua & Barbuda at their own leisure, renting a car is a well-liked and practical option. This choice gives you the freedom and flexibility to find the numerous undiscovered gems of this Caribbean paradise thanks to the well-maintained road networks and a wide variety of rental companies.

One of the main benefits of hiring a car is having easy access to the less visited, off-the-beaten-path sites that best exhibit Antigua and Barbuda's true natural beauty and cultural diversity. With your own vehicle, you can plan your own itinerary and explore sights and scenic areas on your own time, whether you are visiting the well-known 365 beaches in Antigua or the pink sands of Barbuda.

Compact vehicles, SUVs, and even jeeps are available for rent from companies at Antigua's V.C. Bird International Airport and other key hubs, meeting the different needs of travelers. To guarantee availability and lock in the best prices, it is advised to make reservations in advance, especially during the busiest travel times.

Due to English-language road signs and left-hand driving on the islands, getting about is not too difficult. The typical speed restriction is 40 mph, and seat belt use is required. Although you are permitted to drive using your home country's license, getting an international driving permit is advised for increased convenience and security.

Renting a car in Antigua and Barbuda is a convenient, pleasurable, and comfortable mode of transportation that makes it simple for tourists to maximize their Caribbean experience.

Taxis

In Antigua and Barbuda, taxis are a practical and well-liked method of transportation for locals and tourists touring these Caribbean islands.

At important locations like airports, seaports, and urban regions, taxis are extensively accessible. They are easily identified by their characteristic yellow license plates and provide a dependable mode of transportation. Although the government normally fixes and regulates the rates, it is still a good idea to check the fee with the driver before setting out on your journey.

Taxi drivers frequently serve as amiable and informed tour guides, offering a comfortable and individualized experience. They frequently impart knowledge about the history and culture of the area and even suggest hidden jewels. Taxis are especially practical for travelers who want prompt, door-to-door transportation to their selected locations, whether they are a beach, a restaurant, or a historical site.

Overall, taxis provide a hassle-free and delightful method to discover Antigua and Barbuda's natural beauty and local culture while also taking advantage of the friendliness and hospitality of the local drivers.

Bicycle

In Antigua and Barbuda, bicycles provide an environmentally beneficial and relaxing mode of transportation. The islands are a perfect location for cyclists due to their modest size and picturesque coastal roads. On Antigua and Barbuda, a lot of resorts provide free bicycles to visitors, making it simple to explore the neighborhood. Cycling enables you to take in the breathtaking natural beauty of these Caribbean islands at a leisurely pace, whether you wish to bike along Antigua's 365 beaches, visit historical monuments, or simply take in the magnificent ocean vistas. It is a great way to stay active, take in the calm atmosphere, and engage with the community.

Ferries

For those who want to see both islands, ferries offer a convenient and beautiful way to travel around Antigua and Barbuda. These quick boat rides provide a distinctive viewpoint of the Caribbean islands. They run between Antigua and Barbuda, enabling travelers to travel between the two islands and take in each one's unique charms. Regular services are provided by several ferry operators, making island hopping convenient and entertaining. For day trips or longer stays, ferries are a popular option. They offer a peaceful and picturesque journey, complete with breathtaking coastal vistas and the cooling sea breeze, which adds to the charm of discovering this tropical paradise.

Private Yachts and Charter Boats

The gorgeous islands of Antigua and Barbuda can be explored in style and exclusivity on private yachts and charter boats. These boats offer a distinctive approach to explore the Caribbean paradise, which boasts a coastline decorated with quiet coves, spotless beaches, and crystal-clear waters.

Private charters are the pinnacle of freedom and flexibility for people looking for customized, one-of-a-kind experiences.

By choosing the locations and activities that best suit their interests, travelers can create their own itineraries. Private yachts and charter boats provide you the freedom to create the perfect island trip, whether you are looking for undiscovered beaches, brilliant coral reefs for snorkeling, or distant anchorages for peace and quiet.

These boats provide a variety of alternatives to suit different preferences, from family-friendly excursions to romantic sunset cruises. Additionally, they offer a chance to explore the nearby cays and islets, each of which has an own personality and allure. Aboard these boats, Antigua and Barbuda truly come to life as you cruise over the sparkling Caribbean waterways, providing an incredible tour through a tropical paradise.

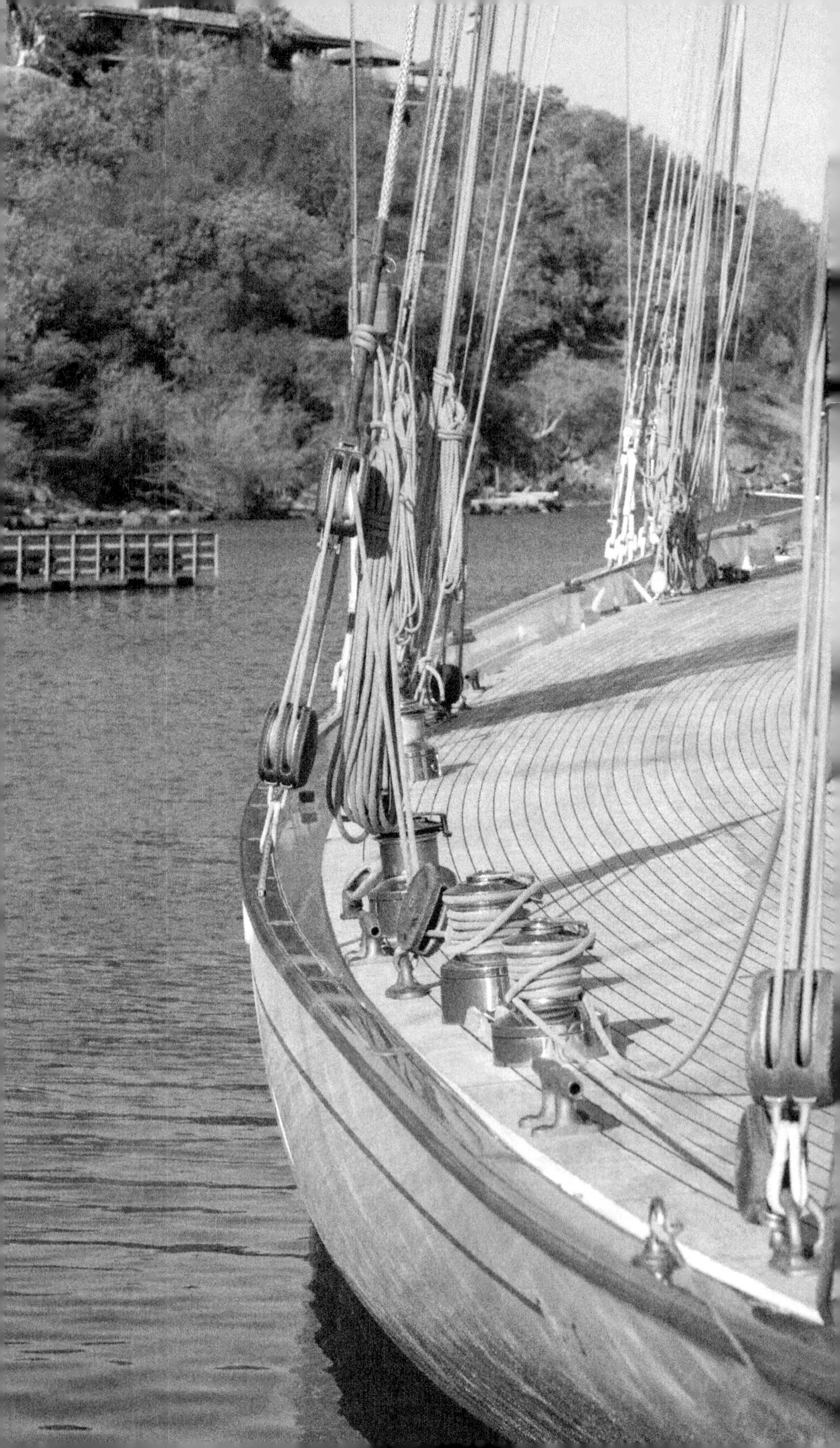

CHAPTER 8

OUTDOOR ACTIVITIES AND ADVENTURE

Beaches in Antigua and Barbuda

The beaches on Antigua and Barbuda are world-famous, and Antigua is frequently referred to as having "365 beaches," which is believed to be one beach for each day of the year. There are many beautiful beaches scattered around the islands, though the precise number may vary depending on how one defines a particular beach. Contrarily, Barbuda has somewhat fewer beaches than Antigua, yet they are no less alluring. These beaches range in size, shape, and personality, allowing everyone a choice between lively, crowded beaches and peaceful, quiet coves. The vast coastline of Antigua and Barbuda offers a variety of beach activities to enjoy, whether you are looking for exciting water sports and entertainment or quiet leisure.

Beaches in Antigua

An astounding variety of beaches, each with a special appeal, can be found in Antigua. Although it is difficult to present an entire list, here are some of Antigua's busiest and most well-known beaches.

Dickenson Bay Beach: this is one of the busiest and most well-known beaches on the island, and it is close to St. John's.

Runaway Beach: Located next to Dickenson Bay, it has lovely white sand and a calmer ambiance.

Jabberwock Beach: It is a favorite spot for kiteboarders and windsurfers on the northeastern coast.

Pigeon Point Beach: This beach, which is close to English Harbour, is well-known for its old sites.

Darkwood Beach: Situated on the west coast, Darkwood Beach is renowned for its peace and tranquility and calm waves.

Half Moon Bay: The eastern coast's Half Moon Bay is well known for its natural beauty and coral reefs.

Galleon Beach: This beach is close to Nelson's Dockyard and is tucked away within English Harbour.

Valley Church Beach: This beach is situated on the west coast and is well-known for its tranquil seas and stunning sunsets.

Ffryes Beach: This beach, which is close to Jolly Harbour, is well-known for its picturesque palm trees.

Morris Bay: This is a hidden gem with peaceful surroundings that may be found on the southern coast.

Nonsuch Bay Beach: On the eastern shore lies a beach called Nonsuch Bay Beach, which is renowned for its serenity and natural beauty.

Long Bay: Long Bay is a vast stretch of white sand in the northeast that is perfect for strolls.

Galley Bay Beach: This quiet beach is the location of the Galley Bay Resort.

Beaches in Barbuda

While the smaller island of Barbuda does not have as many beaches as Antigua, it does provide a distinctive and peaceful beach experience. Some of Barbuda's well-known beaches are listed below:

Pink Sand Beach: Possibly Barbuda's most well-known beach, it is noted for its gorgeous pink sand, crystal-clear seas, and peaceful tranquility.

Coco Point Beach: On Barbuda's southernmost point is Coco Point Beach, a serene area renowned for its stunning beach and clear waters.

Princess Diana Beach: which is located on the northwest coast and was named in memory of the late Princess Diana, is well-known for its immaculate white sand.

Gravenor Bay: On the eastern shore is Gravenor Bay, a tranquil beach and excellent place to see birds.

Low Bay: This is another beach on Barbuda's western shore with pinkish sand and the island's famed turquoise seas.

Spanish Point Beach: This is a great place for picnicking and bird watching because it is close to the lagoon.

Cedar Tree Point Beach: On the northwest coast, Cedar Tree Point Beach offers excellent sandy shoreline and breathtaking views.

Cavalier Beach: This is a tranquil retreat on the southwest coast of the country.

Water sports

In addition to its magnificent beaches and green surroundings, the Caribbean country of Antigua and Barbuda is also known for its growing water sports industry. These islands are a sanctuary for water sports aficionados thanks to their turquoise waters, consistent trade winds, and mild tropical climate.

The most popular water sport in Antigua and Barbuda is sailing. Numerous sailing competitions, including the renowned Antigua Sailing Week, are held on the islands. This occasion exhibits the sailors' and spectators' enthusiasm for the sport on the islands. Both novice and expert sailors can enjoy sailing in the protected coves like Falmouth and

English Harbours. To explore the coasts and offshore cays, guests can rent boats or enroll in sailing courses.

Due to the regular trade winds, windsurfing and kiteboarding are also common pastimes. Both novices and specialists may enjoy gliding across the waves thanks to the numerous rental facilities and schools along the shore. Scuba diving and snorkeling are also must-try activities for seeing the abundant marine life and underwater wrecks. Famous dive destinations like Cades Reef and the Pillars of Hercules provide breath-taking underwater experiences.

Kayaking and paddle boarding are great options for anyone looking for a more relaxed water experience. Enjoy the natural splendor of the island while exploring the tranquil mangroves and secret coves. Also, do not forget about the exhilarating powerboat tours, where you may cruise across the water and stop at isolated beaches for a unique view of Antigua & Barbuda's coastline.

Antigua and Barbuda are a great place for aquatic adventures because water sports there are accessible to people of all ages and ability levels. These islands provide a lively and diverse range of water-based sports, all set against some of the most stunning coastline scenery in the world, whether you're an adrenaline junkie looking for windswept excitement or a family wanting a peaceful day on the water.

Hiking and Nature Excursions

The breathtaking landscapes and rich wildlife of the islands are also showcased by the variety of hiking and nature trips available in Antigua and Barbuda.

Hiking Paths

Antigua and Barbuda provide a network of paths for hikers of all skill levels. On Antigua, the Shirley Heights Lookout Trail is one of the most well-liked walks. It has panoramic views of English and Falmouth Harbours and leads to a historic military complex, giving it a prime location to take in breath-taking sunsets. Boggy Peak, Antigua's highest peak, offers hikers a rewarding summit experience and breathtaking views of the island for a more difficult trip.

The Frangipani Trail and Two Foot Bay Caves are two of the natural treasures that Barbuda has to offer. The Two Foot Bay Caves are a natural wonder with underground limestone caverns and Amerindian rock art, while the Frangipani Trail leads you through lush flora to a serene beach lined with frangipani trees.

Nature Excursions

Travelers interested in nature can explore Antigua and Barbuda's distinctive ecosystems. The largest colony of frigate birds in the Western Hemisphere can be found in the Codrington Lagoon National Park on the island of Barbuda, which is an important haven for birdwatchers. The endangered Hawksbill sea turtle relies on the park as a critical nesting site.

Visitors to Antigua's Donkey Sanctuary can engage with rescued donkeys in a peaceful natural setting, which is a touching experience. The Botanical Gardens of Antigua offer a wide variety of plant species, including orchids, palms, and exotic tropical trees, for individuals who are interested in tropical flora.

A chance to experience the natural beauty of the islands and see marine life like stingrays, turtles, and tropical fish is also provided through boat trips and Eco-adventures to Barbuda's Pink Sand Beach and the Mangroves of Barbuda.

The untouched beauty and vast ecological diversity of Antigua and Barbuda are perfectly accessible through hiking and nature trips. These islands have a multitude of outdoor experiences to offer, whether you are an experienced hiker, a birdwatcher, or simply a nature lover, all set against a backdrop of magnificent Caribbean vistas and serene peacefulness.

Golfing

Golf courses of the highest caliber can be found on both islands, each with a stunning coastline backdrop and a difficult course design.

One of the top golf locations in the area is the Cedar Valley Golf Club in Antigua. Amidst luxuriant tropical foliage, this 18-hole, par-70 course is in the middle of the island. The ocean and the picturesque island hills are visible to golfers in this location. A popular among golfers of all ability levels, the course has a combination of long fairways, little greens, and well-placed bunkers.

Karl Litten created the 18-hole, par-71 Jolly Harbour Golf Club, which is also located in Antigua. The layout is difficult, and the greens are kept up properly. With breathtaking views of the port and the surrounding hills, the course weaves its way around a marina.

The unique 9-hole, par-36 Coco Point Lodge Golf Course is located on the island of Barbuda and is a favorite among golfers. It provides a unique golfing experience with sand greens and a laid-back environment that is ideal for a leisurely round.

A round of golf in Antigua and Barbuda is an amazing experience because of the beautiful scenery, blue waterways, lush surroundings, and warm tropical climate.

CHAPTER 9

CULTURAL EXPERIENCES AND NIGHT LIFE

Annual Celebrations

The annual celebrations of Antigua and Barbuda are known for being vibrant and varied. These occasions showcase the rich history, culture, and spirit of the islands and give residents and guests alike the chance to take part in the vivacious customs that define this area.

1. **Antigua Sailing Week (April/May):** This well-known event attracts sailors from all over the world. It takes place in late April or early May and involves exhilarating boat races set against Antigua's breathtaking shoreline. This regatta is not just a competitive event, but also a time for celebrations with live music, beach parties, and a buzzing atmosphere that penetrates the island.

2. **The Antigua Carnival (July/August):** The Antigua Carnival is the apex of the island's cultural events. It lasts for many weeks and features spectacular costume parades, calypso contests, and beauty pageants. The "Carnival Monday" and "Carnival Tuesday" parades are unmatched in their excitement and ingenuity, with revelers donning vibrant costumes and dancing to the contagious beats of soca and calypso music.

3. **Barbuda Caribana (June):** The sibling festival to Antigua Carnival, Barbuda Caribana is celebrated with equal fervor. With local artists, beauty contests, and lively street parades, it provides a look into the distinctive culture of Barbuda.

4. **Independence Day:** November 1st is Independence Day, which commemorates Antigua and Barbuda's independence from British colonial rule. Parades, cultural displays, and the hoisting of the flag are used to mark the occasion. It is an opportunity to learn about the nation's transition to self-government.

5. **Wadadli Day (November 1):** This national holiday honors Antigua's distinct culture and tradition and falls on the same day as Independence Day. Cultural displays highlighting regional artwork, music, and culinary customs are also part of it.

6. **Christmas and New Year's celebrations:** The holiday season in Antigua and Barbuda is characterized by merry decorations, Christmas carol singing, and happy reunions. Fireworks and boisterous celebrations are used to ring in the new year, bringing together both residents and tourists.

7. **Green Castle Estate Harvest Festival (October):** This yearly celebration honors Antigua's strong agricultural legacy. It is held at Green Castle Estate and gives guests a chance to pick their own fresh food, eat local fare, and experience island country life. It is a chance to feel a connection to the land and understand the value of agriculture in the area.

8. **Mango Festival (July):** The Mango Festival is a delicious celebration of Antigua and Barbuda's plentiful mango harvest. While consuming a range of foods and beverages with a

mango theme, guests may take in live entertainment and cultural exhibits.

These yearly events in Antigua and Barbuda serve as both a display for the colorful culture of the islands and an invitation to locals of all backgrounds to take part in the festivities. They offer a glimpse into the warm and hospitable culture of the Caribbean, where joy, music, and celebration are at the core of the neighborhood.

Nightlife

Antigua and Barbuda's nightlife are a lively and energetic environment that caters to a wide variety of inclinations, from relaxed seaside pubs to explosive dance clubs. These Caribbean islands offer the perfect setting for enjoying the warm, tropical evenings and the local culture after the sun goes down.

Beach Bars: The beach bar scene is one of Antigua and Barbuda's most well-known attractions. OJ's Beach Bar, Castaways, and Jacqui O's Beach House are just a few examples of beachfront businesses that provide the classic

Caribbean nightlife experience. With your toes in the sand, you can indulge in tropical cocktails, sip on rum punch, or drink local beer here. It is the perfect place for a laid-back evening beneath the stars because of the casual environment and frequent live music performances.

Shirley Heights Lookout: Both locals and tourists should visit Shirley Heights Lookout on Sunday evenings. This former military facility offers amazing views of the setting sun across English and Falmouth Harbours. Highlights include live reggae and steelpan music, BBQ, and a buzzing, social environment at the weekly Shirley Heights party.

St. John's Nightlife: There are many ways to spend the night in the nation's capital. There is something for everyone, from hip cocktail bars like Hemingway's Caribbean Café to lively bars like Abracadabra Nightclub. After dusk, St. John's comes to life as locals and visitors mingle, dance to Caribbean beats and savor the island's famous rum concoctions.

Live Music: The music scene in Antigua and Barbuda is booming. At multiple locations throughout the islands, you may see live performances of a variety of genres, including reggae, calypso, soca, and steel-pan. Talented local musicians frequently perform at beach-side bars, resorts, and even street vendors, fostering a laid-back and enjoyable ambiance.

Full Moon Parties: Some beach side venues hold amazing full moon parties on specific nights, particularly during full moons. These events frequently feature bonfires, upbeat music, dancing, and a sense of community that unites individuals from many backgrounds to rejoice beneath the moonlight.

Casinos: Antigua features casinos, including King's Casino in St. John's, for those looking for a little gaming action. They provide an alternate kind of nocturnal entertainment by offering a variety of games, such as poker and slot machines.

CHAPTER 10

DINING AND CUISINE

Local Food and Specialties

A fusion of African, Caribbean, and European influences may be found in the thriving culinary scene of Antigua and Barbuda. These islands' native cuisine and specialty are a true reflection of their extensive natural riches and rich cultural past. Here are a some of the delectable local specialties to try while visiting Antigua & Barbuda:

1. **Fungus:** A mainstay of Antiguan cuisine, fungus is a polenta-like dish made of cornmeal and okra. It is frequently served with fried fish or saltfish (salted codfish). It is a well-liked comfort dish because of the marriage of flavors and textures.

2. **Pepperpot:** Made with a variety of meats, veggies, and spices, pepperpot is a substantial stew with Amerindian origins. Although it can be obtained all year round, it is typically consumed as a Christmas custom and is slow-cooked.

3. **Dukuna:** Also known as tie-a-leaf, dukuna is a tasty dish that is wrapped in banana leaves and steam-cooked to perfection using grated sweet potatoes, coconut, and spices.

Popular as a snack or side dish, saltfish is frequently served with it.

4. **Fungee and Pepperpot:** Fungee is a type of food that resembles fungus but is made from cornmeal and eaten with a flavorful and hearty pepperpot sauce. This filling and substantial dish has a long history on the island.

5. **Saltfish with Johnny Cakes:** Johnny Cakes are fried dumplings that are frequently mixed with saltfish, a well-liked and adaptable delicacy. The savory-sweet combination is a well-liked brunch or breakfast choice.

6. **Seafood Delights:** Given that Antigua and Barbuda are bordered by the Caribbean Sea, it is not surprising that seafood plays a significant role in local cuisine. There are many ways to prepare fresh catches like lobster, conch, and different types of seafood, from grilling and frying to curries and stews.

7. **Goat Water:** This tasty stew, which has become a local favorite, is cooked with goat meat, breadfruit, veggies, and a variety of seasonings.

8. **Roti:** A favorite dish in Antigua and Barbuda, roti is a product of Indian influence in the Caribbean. It comprises of flatbread stuffed with chicken, goat, or veggies cooked in curry. It is a tasty, portable supper that is frequently eaten on the go.

9. **Pineapple Chicken:** This dish, a delectable fusion of sweet and savory, contains soft chicken cooked with pineapple and a combination of spices, creating a tantalizing combination that is a testament to the tropical delicacies of the islands.

10. **Local Desserts:** If you have a sweet taste, Antigua and Barbuda has some delicious desserts to offer, like sugar cake, a sweet treat made from coconut and sugar, and tamarind balls, a tart treat made from tamarind pulp and sugar.

11. **Local Drinks:** Don't miss the chance to try some local drinks, like the renowned rum from Antigua and Barbuda, which is renowned for its great quality. Enjoy freshly squeezed fruit juices prepared from exotic fruits including mango, guava, and passion fruit.

Local cuisine and specialties in Antigua and Barbuda provide a delicious tour through the history and flavors of the islands.

Restaurants and Cafes

There are many different types of food to choose from in Antigua and Barbuda, from traditional Caribbean fare to cosmopolitan cuisine. Here are a few eateries that perfectly represent the mouthwatering dining options on these Caribbean islands:

1. **Sheer Rocks, Antigua:** This culinary wonder is perched on the rocks above Ffryes Beach. The eatery provides a Caribbean-inspired menu with Mediterranean influences. It is the perfect place for a romantic evening because guests may enjoy their supper on plush daybeds or beside the infinity pool.

2. **Cecelia's High Point Café, Barbuda:** Visit Cecelia's High Point Café for a quaint and genuine experience on Barbuda. This family-run restaurant serves up regional seafood specialties, authentic Caribbean cuisine, and breathtaking island panoramas.

3. **Pillars Restaurant, Antigua:** This historic eatery is housed at the Admiral's Inn at Nelson's Dockyard. The menu combines European and Caribbean flavors, and diners may take advantage of the lovely courtyard environment while they are eating.

4. **Papa Zouk, Antigua:** Papa Zouk is a well-known seafood restaurant in St. John's that seafood fans will not want to miss. This is the place to go for a true taste of Caribbean seafood, with a relaxed ambiance and a wide variety of fresh catches.

5. **Dennis Cocktail Bar & Restaurant, Antigua:** For many years, this venerable restaurant in St. John's has served authentic Antiguan food. It is a must-visit for both visitors and residents due to the inviting atmosphere and the menu's inclusion of regional specialties like saltfish and fungee.

6. **Le Bistro Restaurant, Antigua:** Le Bistro is a good pick for French food with a Caribbean twist. It provides great meals in a romantic environment and is situated within the Blue Waters Resort.

7. **Big Banana, Antigua:** This well-liked eatery in St. John's is renowned for its relaxed ambiance and varied food. It is a terrific place to eat comfort food from the United States and the Caribbean and take in the vibrant nightlife.

8. **Le Colibri Restaurant, Antigua:** The quaint French-Caribbean restaurant Le Colibri in Antigua serves delectable French cuisine in a romantic garden setting. It is perfect for an elegant evening or festive occasion.

9. **Island Fusion, Barbuda:** Island Fusion is a relaxed cafe that serves delectable seafood dishes, sandwiches, and

energizing drinks. It is a great location to chill and take in the laid-back vibe of the island.

10. **Hemingway's Caribbean Café, Antigua:** This renowned hangout is in St. John's and is frequented by both locals and visitors. It is renowned for its live music, beverages, and extensive menu that includes both Caribbean and foreign cuisine.

These are just a few examples of Antigua & Barbuda's many dining alternatives. These islands offer a culinary experience that complements their spectacular natural beauty and vibrant culture, ranging from seaside cafes selling fresh seafood to upmarket restaurants serving great international cuisine.

CHAPTER 11

SHOPPING AND SOUVENIRS

Local Markets

The best way to experience the genuine culture and energetic atmosphere of Antigua and Barbuda is by exploring the local markets there. Here is a sample of what you may anticipate discovering from locally sourced foods to fresh produce to handcrafted goods:

1. **Saturday Morning Market in St. John's:** The vibrant Saturday Morning Market in St. John's, the nation's capital, is a popular destination for both locals and tourists. Fresh fruits, vegetables, spices, and a range of regional goods are all available for purchase here. Live music enhances the dynamic environment, making it a lively and fun experience.

2. **Heritage Quay in St. John's:** This duty-free retail district in St. John's offers a variety of handicrafts, jewelry, apparel,

and souvenirs made locally. Tourists frequently go there in search of one-of-a-kind souvenirs and gifts.

3. **Redcliffe Quay in St. John's:** A short distance away from Heritage Quay, Redcliffe Quay provides a similar selection of boutiques and art galleries for shopping. Your shopping excursion will be in a wonderful atmosphere thanks to the charming architecture and cobblestone streets.

4. **Street Vendors in St. John's:** There are many street vendors in St. John's that sell fresh fruit, regional foods, and handcrafted crafts. This is a great chance to interact with regional craftspeople and enjoy real Caribbean cuisine.

5. **Public Market, St. John's:** The Public Market in St. John's is a center of community activity where you can buy local specialties including fresh fruits and vegetables and spices. It is a great location to witness daily life on the island and become immersed in the colorful market culture.

6. **Farmers' Markets in Barbuda:** The island's culinary scene in Barbuda is centered on the neighborhood farmers' markets. These sporadic markets offer the chance to buy fresh food, local crafts, and other products from the growers themselves.

7. **Street Markets in Barbuda:** Barbuda has street markets where a variety of regional goods are sold. Along with traditional food from Antigua and Barbuda, you may find mementos and artwork there. Supporting regional craftspeople and enjoying island tastes are both opportunities provided by these marketplaces.

8. **Craft and Art Markets:** You may find craft and art markets on both islands, where regional artisans can display their skills. Unique paintings, sculptures, jewelry, and other

handcrafted items are available and make excellent gifts or souvenirs.

Discovering the local markets in Antigua and Barbuda gives you the chance to not only purchase for genuine, locally sourced goods but also to interact with the welcoming locals and get a taste of the vibrant local culture.

Handcrafted Goods

These islands are a veritable gold mine of regional crafts that showcase the distinct Caribbean culture and tradition. Here is a look at some of the locally made goods available in Antigua & Barbuda:

1. **Antiguan and Barbudan Pottery:** The beautiful and practical pottery made by local artisans frequently features elaborate designs and brilliant colors. Antigua and Barbuda's pottery ranges from beautiful bowls and vases to dinnerware and is both creative and functional.

2. **Basketry:** It is usual to see handwoven baskets made of materials like sweet grass, bamboo, and coconut fibers. These

baskets, which come in a variety of sizes and forms, can be used both as useful storage containers and as lovely ornamental accents.

3. **Batik textiles:** Using a traditional dying method, batik produces intricate and vibrant fabric designs. This technique is used by local artists in Antigua and Barbuda to produce distinctive clothes, accessories, and home decor products.

4. **Hand-Painted Art:** Skilled creators create magnificent works of art that perfectly represent the vivacious character of the islands. Their artwork frequently features seascapes

and tropical landscapes, as well as the vibrant culture of Antigua and Barbuda.

1. **Jewelry:** The natural beauty of the Caribbean serves as inspiration for the creators of distinctive jewelry. Shells, semi-precious stones, coral, and more can be used to create necklaces, earrings, bracelets, and other jewelry.

2. **Woodwork:** Skilled woodworkers create a range of products, from modest decorative items to furniture with sophisticated designs. For dramatic effects, the natural warmth of wood is frequently blended with the Caribbean's brilliant colors.

3. **Hammocks and Textiles:** Handwoven by native artists, hammocks, rugs, and textiles not only serve a practical purpose but also highlight the artistic talent of the islands. These things are ideal for giving your house a hint of the Caribbean.

4. **Shell Art:** Stunning artwork and decorative objects are made from seashells that are collected from Antigua and

Barbuda's beaches. These local crafts, which range from mosaics to picture frames covered in shells, are distinctive.

9. **Carved Calabash Gourds:** Local artists expertly carve calabash gourds with exquisite designs and patterns to create musical instruments, bowls, and other decorative items.

10. **Beading:** Local artists create beaded jewelry and accessories in a range of colors and designs. Handcrafted beading is a well-liked art form.

Many of these homemade items are offered in neighborhood markets, craft stores, and even directly from the craftsmen, giving shoppers the chance to purchase one-of-a-kind and genuine items. Antigua and Barbuda's handicraft history not only preserves the local culture and traditions but also gives tourists an opportunity to bring a piece of the bright and creative spirit of the islands home.

Duty-Free Shopping

A shopper's paradise, Antigua and Barbuda offers duty-free shopping. These stunning Caribbean islands provide a wide range of duty-free products, from luxury goods to regional goods, giving visitors a fantastic opportunity to buy high-quality goods at more reasonable costs. A closer look at Antigua and Barbuda's duty-free shopping is provided below:

1. **Duty-Free Jewelers And Watch Shops:** Antigua and Barbuda are well known for their duty-free jewelers. A wide variety of goods are available, including stunning pieces made from priceless metals and diamonds. There are several well-known brands as well as jewelry made specifically for you. Duty-free shopping is a fantastic method to get gorgeous jewelry without paying the additional tax, whether you are looking for engagement rings, exquisite necklaces, or luxury watches.

2. **Alcohol And Tobacco:** A wide variety of duty-free alcoholic beverages, including premium brands of rum, wine, champagne, and other spirits, are available on the islands. This is especially tempting considering how well-known Antigua and Barbuda are for making rum. Additionally, visitors have the option of paying competitive prices for duty-free tobacco products including cigars and cigarettes.

3. **Cosmetics And Scents:** The duty-free shops on the islands provide a great assortment of cosmetics and scents. Whether you are looking for a signature aroma, luxury skincare items, or high-end beauty brands, you will discover a wide selection at budget-friendly pricing.

4. **Designer Fashion:** Antigua and Barbuda are home to duty-free shops that sell accessories and clothing from top designers. These shops provide a chance to indulge in high-end fashion without the usual import fees, offering anything from fashionable clothing to opulent handbags and sunglasses.

5. **Electronics:** Those who love technology will appreciate the duty-free electronics shops, which provide a variety of

items at affordable costs, including cameras, smartphones, computers, and other gadgets. This is especially useful for travelers looking for amazing deals on the newest technology or in need of last-minute equipment.

6. **Local Souvenirs:** Duty-free shops frequently provide locally produced goods like handicrafts, fabrics, and souvenirs in addition to high-end international goods. These products enable visitors to take a bit of the island culture and customs with them when they depart.

5. **Local Specialty Food and Spices:** You can also buy regional specialties like Antiguan Black Pineapple Rum Cake and Antiguan hot sauces in duty-free shops. You can also buy a variety of Caribbean spices to give your meals back home a taste of the islands.

Because there are no import taxes or sales taxes on the commodities, duty-free shopping in Antigua and Barbuda is very alluring because you may frequently save a lot of money. Both islands include duty-free-specific shopping areas and malls, making for an easy and delightful shopping experience.

CHAPTER 12

PLANNING YOUR ITINERARY

5 Days Itinerary

To make the most of your trip to these stunning Caribbean islands, consider the following 5-day itinerary:

Day 1: Arriving to Antigua

- Welcome to the Antigua V.C. Bird International Airport.
- Whether it is a posh resort or a quaint boutique hotel, check in to your chosen lodging.
- Relax for the afternoon on one of Antigua's beautiful beaches, such as Dickenson Bay or Runaway Bay.
- In the evening, take in some genuine Caribbean cuisine for a welcome supper at a nearby restaurant.

Day 2: Examine the history and environment of Antigua

- Visit Nelson's Dockyard, a UNESCO World Heritage Site, first thing in the morning to learn more about the rich maritime history of the islands.
- Wander around English Harbor and check out the Dockyard Museum.
- Then, proceed to Shirley Heights Lookout for breathtaking panoramic views and, if it is Sunday night, take in the exciting Shirley Heights Party.
- Visit sights like Wallings Nature Reserve and the rainforest canopy tour as you explore the Fig Tree Drive's paths and beautiful rainforest.
- Once you get back to your lodging, have a leisurely dinner by the water.

Day 3: Day trip to Barbuda

- Take a ferry or a quick trip to Barbuda, the sister island.
- Visit the stunning pink-sand beaches, like Princess Diana Beach, and take a tour of the Frigate Bird Sanctuary.
- Take time to relax and eat lunch on the beach.
- In the late afternoon, return to Antigua, and use the evening to unwind or tour St. John's and its neighborhood markets.

Day 4: Outdoor activities and water sports

- Embark in a day of water sports in Antigua's clear seas. You can go scuba diving, snorkeling, or even paddle-boarding.
- Explore Antigua's coastline and its secret coves by boat.
- Spend the day eating lunch on the beach at one of the island's beach bars.
- Continue your underwater explorations or relax with a good book on the beach.
- For the ideal way to cap off an active day, have dinner by the beach.

Day 5: Leisure and Local Culture
- On your last day in Antigua, spend it relaxing on one of the beaches there, such Jolly Beach or Half Moon Bay.
- Enjoy a beach-side meal or a picnic.
- Shop for trinkets and handcrafted things at local markets.
- Attend a local festival or try some native food at a quaint restaurant in the evening to really experience Antigua's lively culture.
- To make the most of your trip to Antigua and Barbuda, use this 5-day itinerary, which strikes a mix between sightseeing, leisure, and cultural events.

7 Days Itinerary

A 7-day itinerary in Antigua and Barbuda gives you the chance to see these Caribbean islands' colorful culture, breathtaking scenery, and extensive history. Here is a detailed schedule for a remarkable week:

Day 1: Landing into Antigua
- Arrive in Antigua's V.C. Bird International Airport.
- Whether it is a beach-side resort, a boutique hotel, or a lovely villa, check in to your chosen lodging.

- Spend your first evening dining in a neighborhood eatery, indulging in local rum cocktails and Caribbean cuisine.

Day 2: Tour St. John's and its historic sites
- Explore the historic Redcliffe Quay and Heritage Quay for duty-free shopping while in St. John's, the capital of Antigua.
- Discover the stunning architecture of the colonial era at St. John's Cathedral.
- Visit Fort James, a former military outpost with sweeping views of the bay, in the afternoon.
- Unwind on a well-known beach in Antigua, such as Dickenson Bay.

Day 3: Nelson's Dockyard and Shirley Heights
- Spend the morning climbing Shirley Heights for breathtaking views of Falmouth and English Harbours.
- Discover the UNESCO World Heritage Site Nelson's Dockyard, which provides a window into the island's naval past.
- On Sunday afternoons, Shirley Heights comes alive with live music, barbecues, and stunning sunset views.

Day 4: A beach day with water sports

- Visit Half Moon Bay, Pigeon Point, or Darkwood Beach, three of Antigua's most spotless beaches.
- Spend the day swimming, playing in the water, and enjoying water activities like paddle-boarding or snorkeling.
- Lunch on seafood can be had at a coastal eatery.

Day 5: Trip to Barbuda
- Visit Barbuda, Antigua's sister island, for the day.
- Discover the Frigate Bird Sanctuary, the pink sand beaches, and the local culture.
- Enjoy a feast of fresh seafood.
- In the late afternoon, return to Antigua, and spend the evening relaxing at your lodging or visiting St. John's.

Sixth day: adventure and regional culture
- Take part in outdoor activities like hiking to the Wallings Nature Reserve or zip-lining through the rainforest.
- Shop for handmade products and trinkets at local markets.
- Discover the history and culture of the islands by visiting the Antigua and Barbuda Museum in St. John's.
- Attend a neighborhood festival or have dinner at a local Caribbean restaurant in the evening.

Day 7: Relaxed and Goodbye
- On your last day, spend it relaxing at the beach.
- Enjoy a meal by the water or a beach picnic.
- Think back on your trip to the Caribbean while perhaps taking a boat tour of the scenery.

- Enjoy a final meal together as well as a night of dancing and music at a beachfront location.

This 7-day program provides a thorough and varied introduction to Antigua & Barbuda. It includes recreational pursuits, cultural exploration, and lots of leisure time spent on the beautiful beaches of the islands.

CHAPTER 13

PRACTICAL INFORMATION

Tourist Information Centers

To help visitors get the most out of their trip, Antigua and Barbuda has several tourist information centers available. These facilities are created to offer crucial data, maps, brochures, and direction to improve the visiting experience.

There are tourist information centers in Antigua at important areas such Nelson's Dockyard, the cruise ship dock in St. John's, and V.C. Bird International Airport. These resources provide a variety of details, such as information on nearby events, activities, lodging, and transit choices. To ensure you have a wonderful stay, knowledgeable professionals are on hand to respond to queries and offer advice.

The Codrington Village Tourist Information Center in Barbuda is a useful tool for visitors exploring the sister island.

You can learn more about the top beaches, landmarks, and tours on Barbuda right here.

Emergency Contacts

It is important to know who to contact in case of emergency in Antigua and Barbuda:

Emergency Services: In the event of an emergency, dial 911 for immediate assistance from police, firefighters, and ambulances. You can reach all the necessary emergency services by dialing this number.

Antigua and Barbuda Coast Guard: Dial +268 462-0358 to contact the Coast Guard in case of a maritime or coastal emergency.

Hospitals: The Mount St. John's Medical Centre in Antigua is a significant hospital and can be reached at +1 (268) 484-2700 for medical emergencies.

Healthcare in Barbuda: Dial +1 (268) 460-0431 to reach the Holy Trinity Medical Centre in Barbuda.

Local Etiquette and Customs

To have a positive and sensitive cultural experience while visiting Antigua and Barbuda, it's crucial to respect and appreciate the local etiquette and customs:

Greeting: A warm and courteous greeting is required in Antigua and Barbuda. Although a handshake and a grin are customary greetings, using a formal title like "Mr." or "Mrs." is polite.

Respect for Elders: The Caribbean culture places a great priority on respect for elders. When addressing elderly people, use respectful pronouns like "sir" or "ma'am".

Conservative Dress: Although there is a laid-back vibe on the islands, it is still important to wear modestly when you are not at a beach or resort. Both men and women should wear proper clothing, covering shoulders and knees, when attending churches or official institutions.

Punctuality and Greetings: Greetings can be prolonged and include questions about family and general well-being. Being courteous, patient, and making small talk are crucial. Additionally, while being on time is crucial for professional meetings, social events frequently have a lax sense of timing.

Public Displays of Affection: Excessive displays of affection may be construed as disrespectful conduct. thus, they should be maintained to a minimum.

Environmentalism: Antigua and Barbuda are committed to protecting the environment. The natural beauty of the islands should not be harmed by littering.

Photographic advice: Always get permission before taking images of locals or their property, and exercise tact when doing so at revered locations.

Tipping: Tipping is usually appreciated but not required. If a service charge isn't included, it's customary to give a 10-15% tip at restaurants and coffee shops.

Respecting these regional traditions and manners will not only make your trip more enjoyable, but it will also enhance your encounters with the friendly and hospitable people of Antigua and Barbuda.

Currency and Banking

The Eastern Caribbean Dollar, abbreviated as XCD or denoted by the symbol "$," is used as the official currency of Antigua and Barbuda. It is crucial to understand that this currency is distinct from the Eastern Caribbean Dollar used in nations in the Eastern Caribbean Currency Union including Grenada and Saint Lucia. The Eastern Caribbean Dollar has a fixed exchange rate with the US Dollar of 2.70 XCD to 1 USD. Most pricing are listed in both U.S. dollars and Eastern Caribbean Dollars, and U.S. dollars are often accepted.

The banking infrastructure in Antigua and Barbuda is well-established, with lots of banks and ATMs located across the islands, particularly in St. John's, the capital. Most banks provide services such ATM withdrawals, wire transfers, and currency exchange. Hotels, restaurants, and stores frequently take credit cards, especially Visa and Mastercard. Traveler's checks, though less frequent today, can still be cashed at banks and some companies.

To guarantee that your credit and debit cards function properly while you are visiting Antigua and Barbuda, it is advisable to let your bank know about your travel intentions.

Language and Communication

Since English is Antigua and Barbuda's official language, travelers who speak English will have no trouble communicating. As former British colonies, Antigua and Barbuda still speak English as a result of their colonial past. As a result, you will discover that many residents are fluent English speakers and that all government documents, traffic signs, and business transactions are made in English.

Some locals also speak the Antiguan Creole, a regional tongue having African, Caribbean, and English influences, particularly in informal situations. Even though English is the main language spoken, learning a few Creole phrases can be a fun and interesting way to interact with residents and learn about the island's distinctive cultural heritage.

Signs, menus, and educational materials are virtually always available in English when it comes to textual communication.

In Antigua and Barbuda, where tourism is a significant industry, many service personnel are fluent in English. As a result, travelers can easily find their way around the islands and get the information they require to have a positive experience.

Packing Tips

Consider the tropical climate and laid-back ambiance while choosing your travel attire for Antigua and Barbuda. Here are some recommendations for packing:

Light Clothing: Pack breathable, light apparel such as shorts, t-shirts, and sundresses. For comfort in the heat, choose natural textiles like cotton and linen.

Swimwear: Pack many outfits, as you will be spending a lot of time at the beach and in the water.

Sun protection: The sun in the Caribbean can be harsh. To avoid being sunburned, put on high SPF sunscreen, sunglasses, and a wide-brimmed hat.

Insect repellent: Pack insect repellent to prevent bug bites because there may be mosquitoes in the area.

Casual footwear: A pair of walking shoes are excellent for sightseeing, while comfortable flip-flops or sandals are perfect for the beach.

Travel adapters: This are required since Type A and Type B electrical outlets are used in Antigua and Barbuda.

Travel documents: Put your passport, travel insurance, and copies of critical documents in a waterproof bag.

Cash and Credit Cards: Although credit cards are extensively used, having some cash in Eastern Caribbean Dollars on hand for petty transactions can be helpful.

Medication: Bring any prescription medications you require, along with essential OTC meds like antacids and painkillers.

Reusable water bottle: It is important to stay hydrated. Utilizing a reusable water bottle can help you avoid creating unnecessary plastic trash and will keep you hydrated.

In general, travel light, keep things straightforward, and concentrate on taking in Antigua and Barbuda's breathtaking beaches and lively culture.

Safety Tips

Travelers can feel comfortable visiting Antigua & Barbuda. To ensure a worry-free visit, it's crucial to follow a few safety procedures, just like you would anywhere else. These travel safety recommendations are for Antigua and Barbuda:

Water and Beach Safety
- Beach warning flags should be observed. Normally, red flags denote hazardous surf conditions.
- While swimming, snorkeling, or engaging in water activities, use caution. Observe the lifeguard's instructions.

Local laws and ordinances
Observe the customs and laws of the area. In Antigua and Barbuda, several things that are permitted elsewhere might not be allowed there.

Transport Security
- Be cautious on the roads when driving a rental automobile because they can be congested and twisty. Use the left side of the road to drive.
- Use reputable taxi services or regulated transportation providers, and decide on prices in advance of your trip.

Personal Property
- In congested regions and popular tourist destinations, keep an eye on your personal things. Consider anti-theft travel equipment and use zippered bags.

Awareness of the weather
- Watch the weather reports, especially from June to November when hurricanes are expected. Follow any instructions for evacuation if necessary, and be ready.

Environment Respect
- Respect the wildlife and the ecology in the area. While snorkeling or diving, keep your distance from coral reefs and other marine creatures.

CHAPTER 14

CONCLUSION

Useful Phrases

Most locals speak English very well. However, learning a few helpful words and phrases can improve your trip and demonstrate respect for the community's culture. Keep in mind the following words:

Greetings
"Hello" – A straightforward "hello" is an approachable way to begin any conversation.
Use the phrase "good morning" to welcome someone in the morning.
"Good evening" is used during evening interactions.

Local Salutations
"Wah gwan?" - A common salutation that asks, "What's going on?"

"One love" is a phrase that denotes harmony and serenity.

The "Thank You" phrase

"Thank you" - Use this common phrase to express gratitude.

"Cheers" - Frequently used as a jocular manner to express gratitude, particularly in social situations.

Typical Expressions

"No problem" is a casual way of stating "It's okay" or "You're welcome."

"Irie" is a phrase that denotes a happy and cheerful world.

Food Ordering

"May I have..." - Begin your courteous request for food or beverages.

Always include the polite phrase "please" to your requests.

"Check, please" is the phrase you say when you are ready to pay at a restaurant.

Moving About

"Where is..." - Helpful for getting instructions or locating a certain place.

"How much is..." - Useful for finding out costs.

Maps

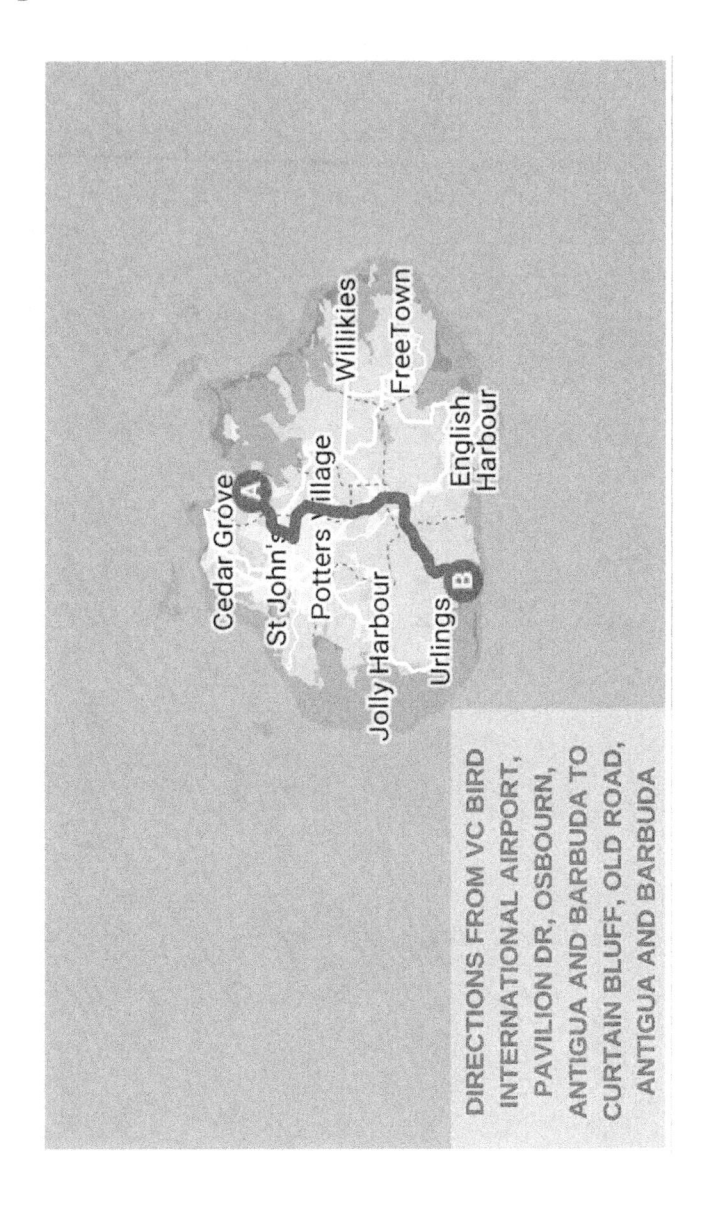

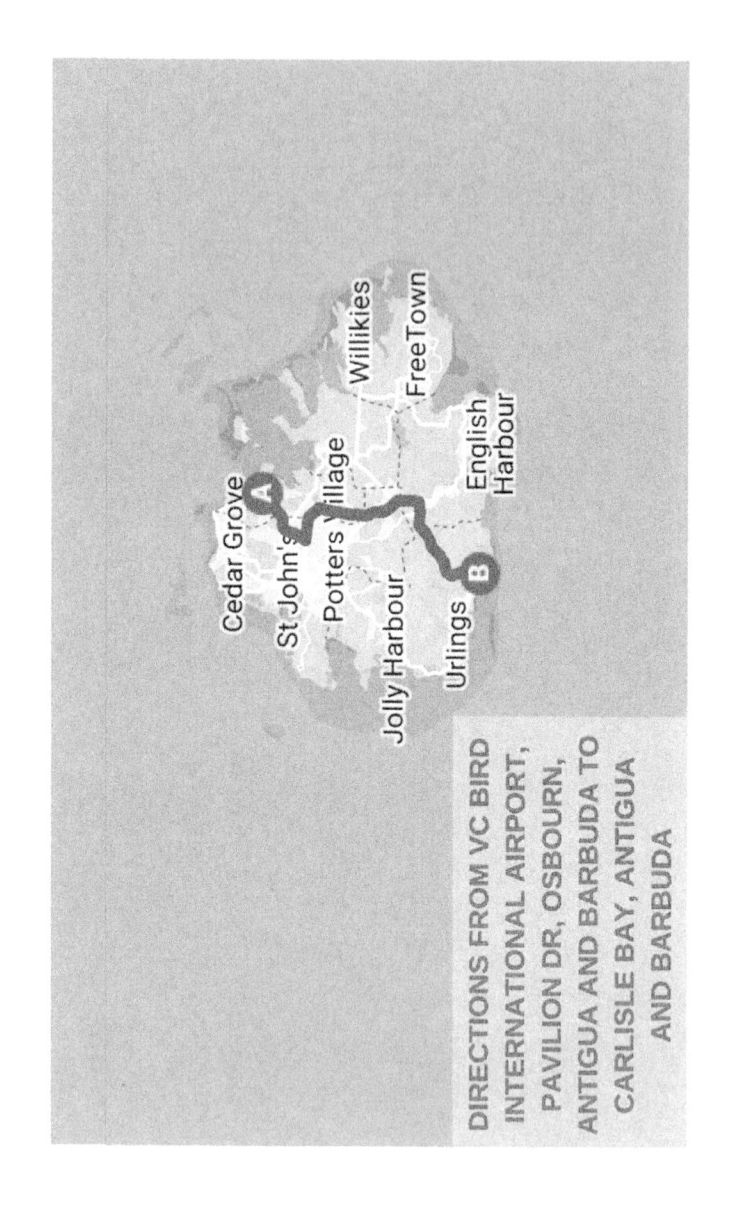

DIRECTIONS FROM VC BIRD INTERNATIONAL AIRPORT, PAVILION DR, OSBOURN, ANTIGUA AND BARBUDA TO CARLISLE BAY, ANTIGUA AND BARBUDA

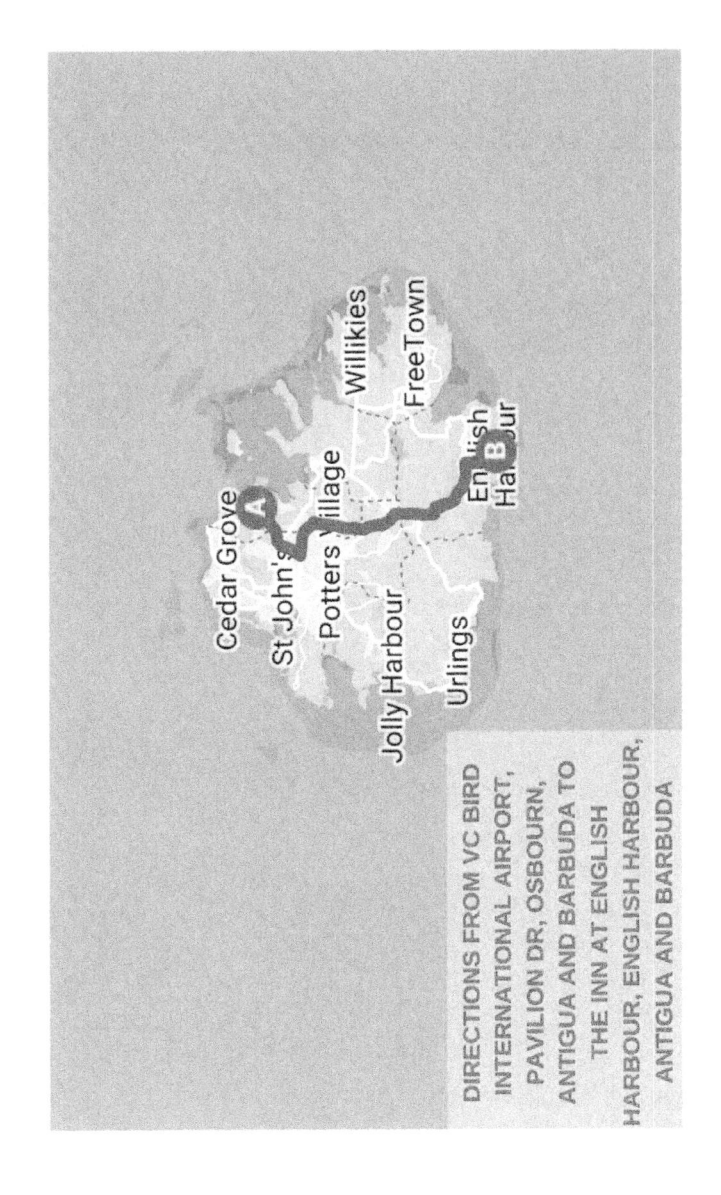

DIRECTIONS FROM VC BIRD INTERNATIONAL AIRPORT, PAVILION DR, OSBOURN, ANTIGUA AND BARBUDA TO THE INN AT ENGLISH HARBOUR, ENGLISH HARBOUR, ANTIGUA AND BARBUDA

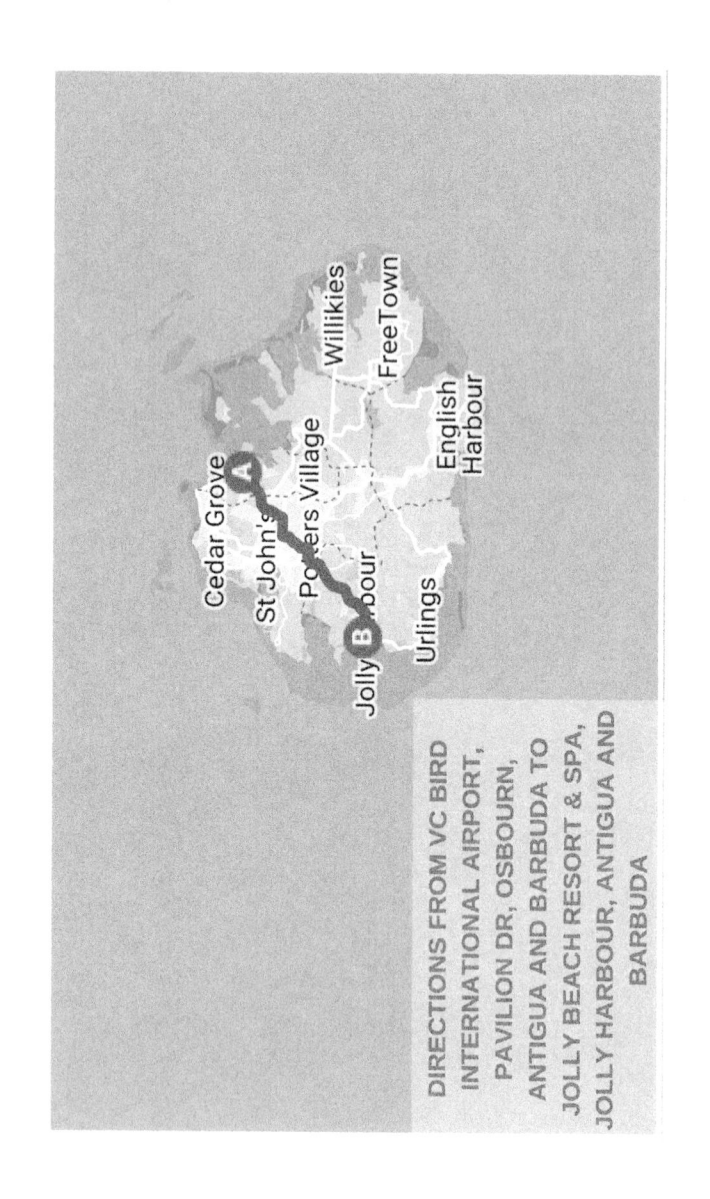

DIRECTIONS FROM VC BIRD INTERNATIONAL AIRPORT, PAVILION DR, OSBOURN, ANTIGUA AND BARBUDA TO JOLLY BEACH RESORT & SPA, JOLLY HARBOUR, ANTIGUA AND BARBUDA

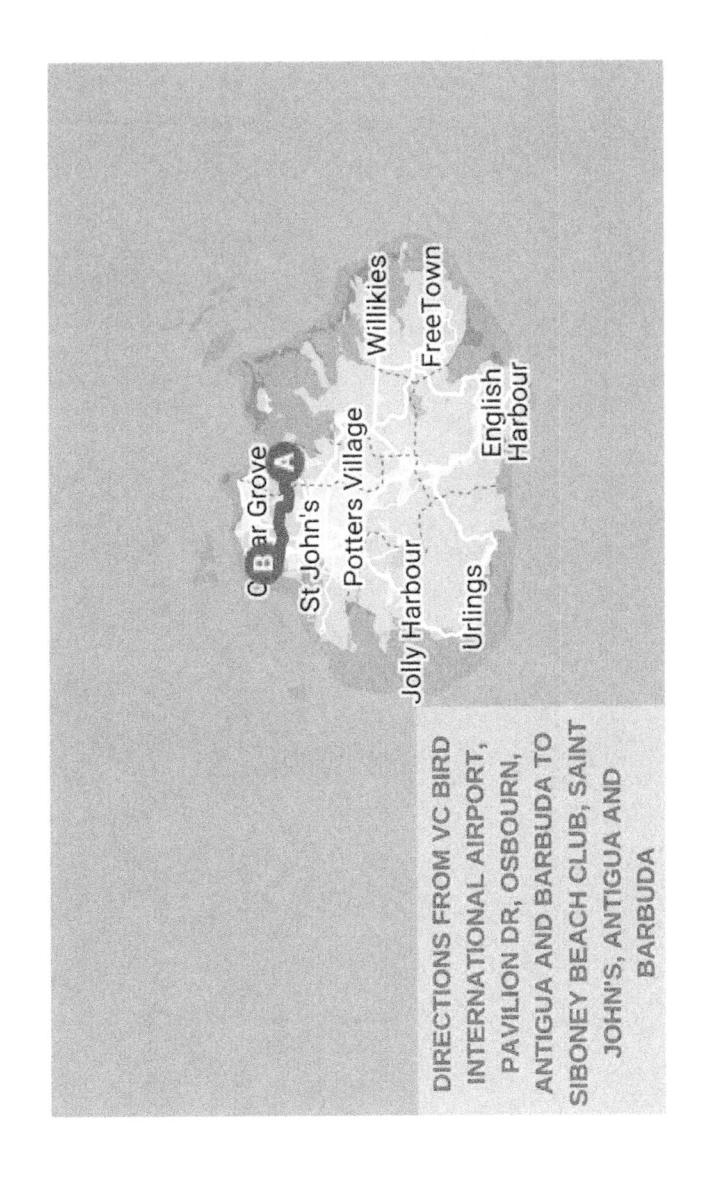

DIRECTIONS FROM VC BIRD INTERNATIONAL AIRPORT, PAVILION DR, OSBOURN, ANTIGUA AND BARBUDA TO SIBONEY BEACH CLUB, SAINT JOHN'S, ANTIGUA AND BARBUDA

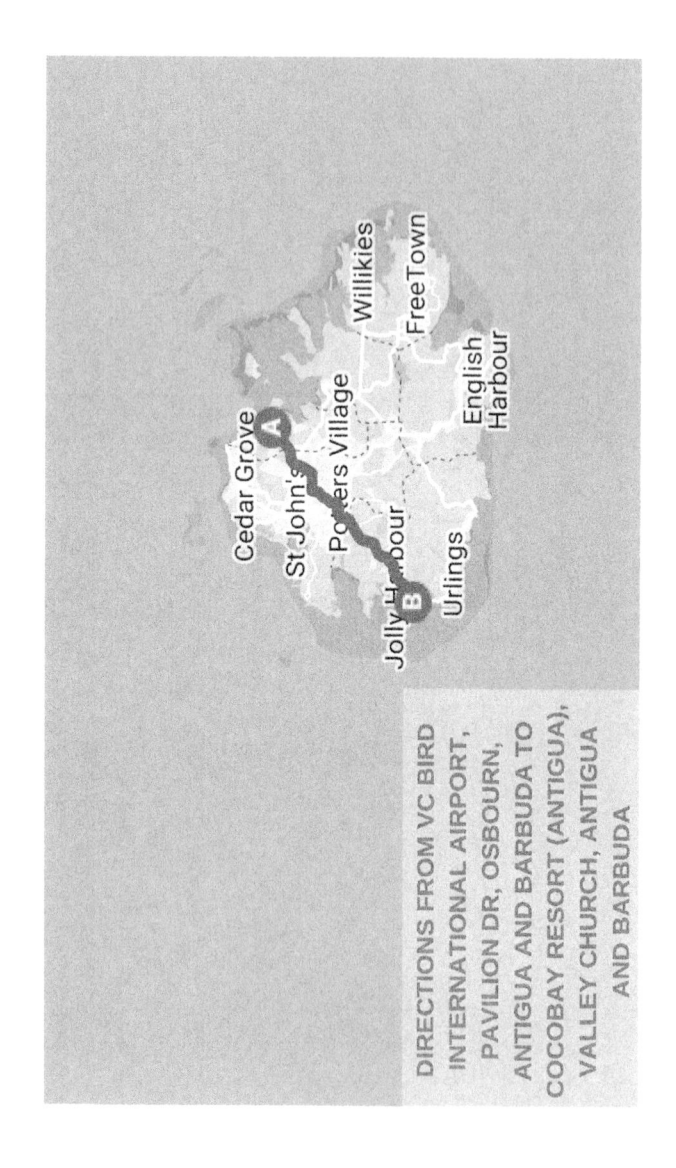

DIRECTIONS FROM VC BIRD INTERNATIONAL AIRPORT, PAVILION DR, OSBOURN, ANTIGUA AND BARBUDA TO COCOBAY RESORT (ANTIGUA), VALLEY CHURCH, ANTIGUA AND BARBUDA

163

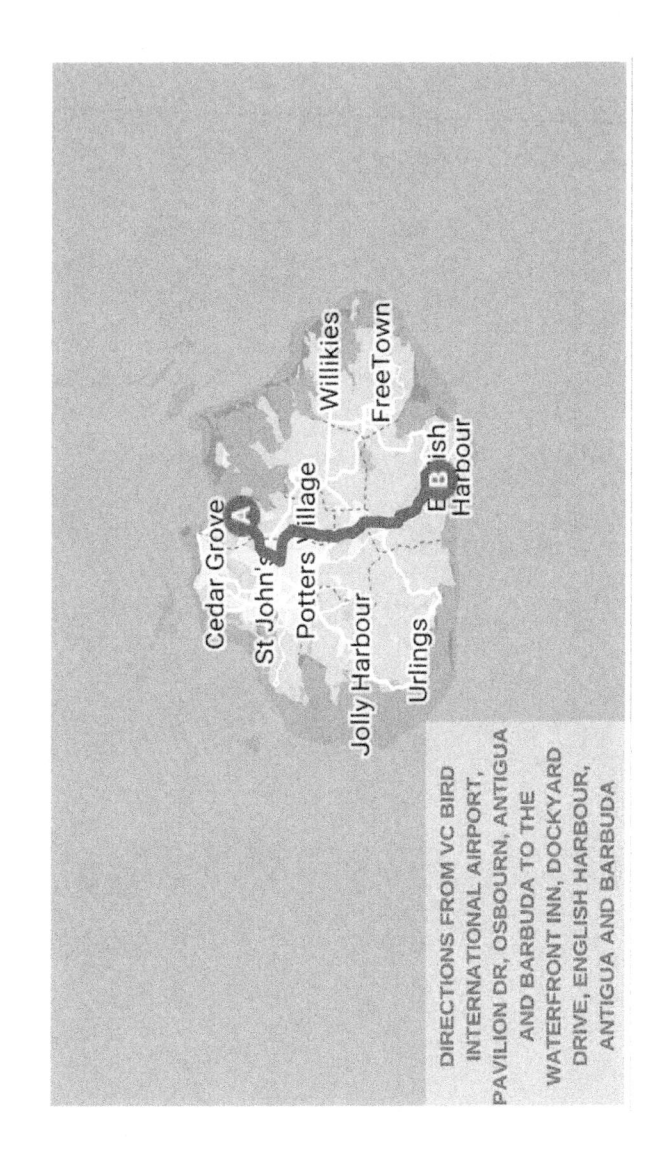

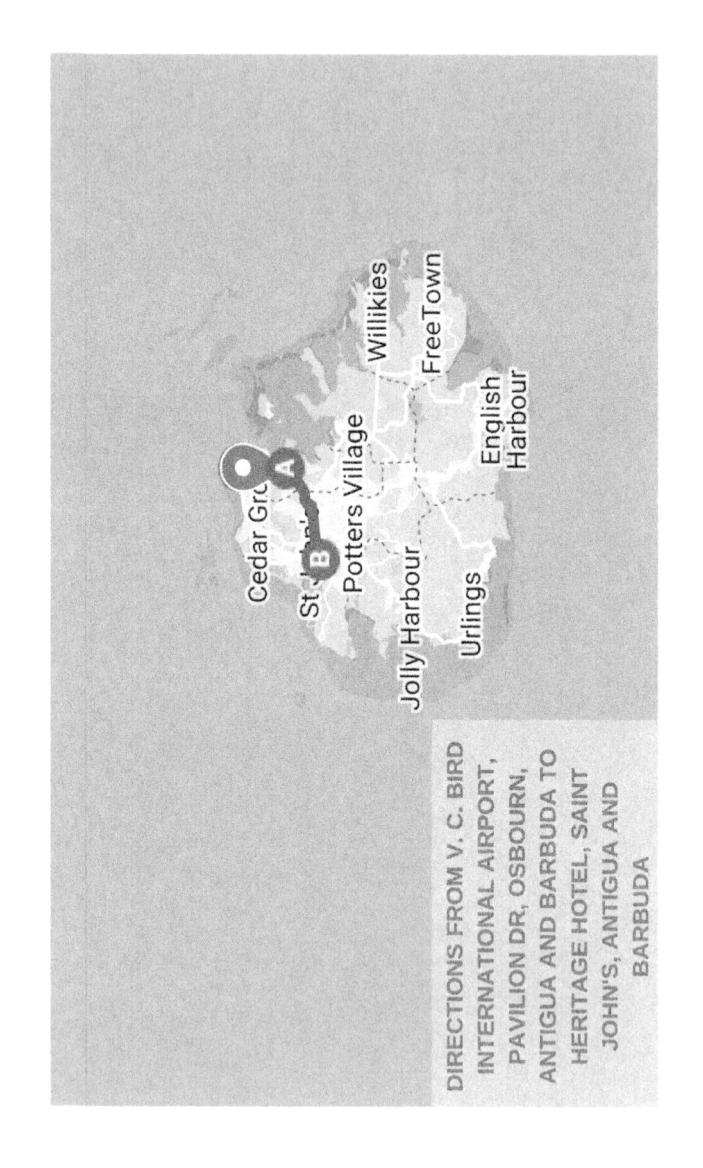

DIRECTIONS FROM V. C. BIRD INTERNATIONAL AIRPORT, PAVILION DR, OSBOURN, ANTIGUA AND BARBUDA TO HERITAGE HOTEL, SAINT JOHN'S, ANTIGUA AND BARBUDA

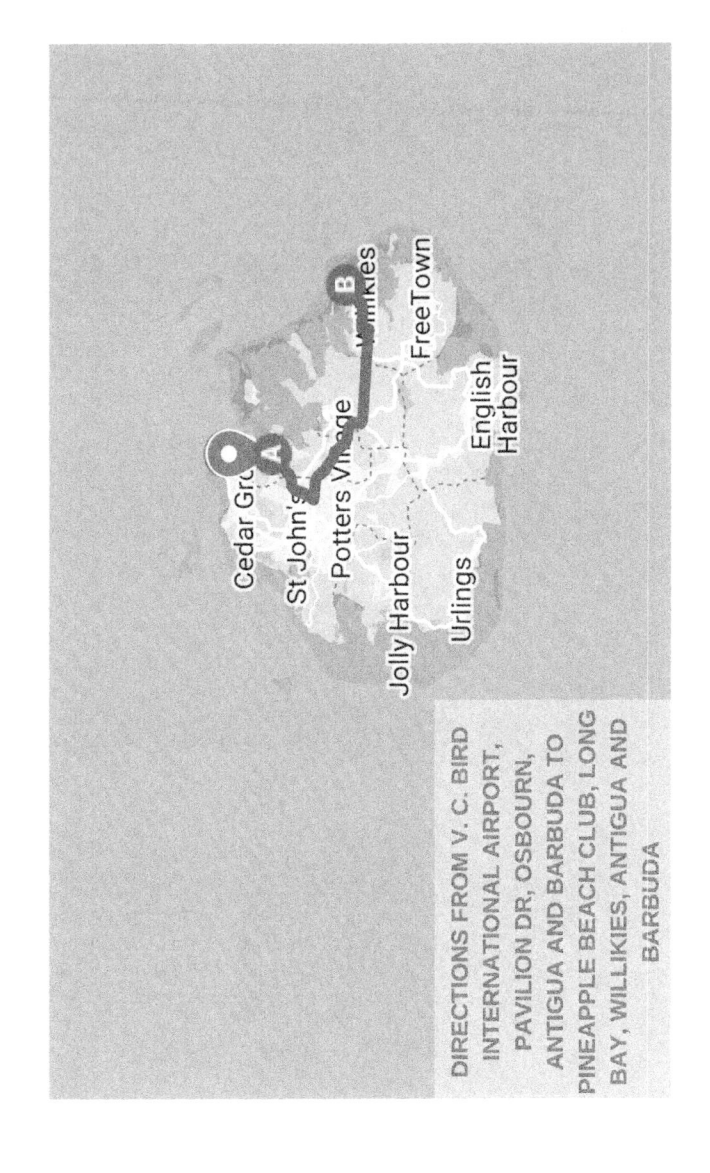

DIRECTIONS FROM V. C. BIRD INTERNATIONAL AIRPORT, PAVILION DR, OSBOURN, ANTIGUA AND BARBUDA TO PINEAPPLE BEACH CLUB, LONG BAY, WILLIKIES, ANTIGUA AND BARBUDA

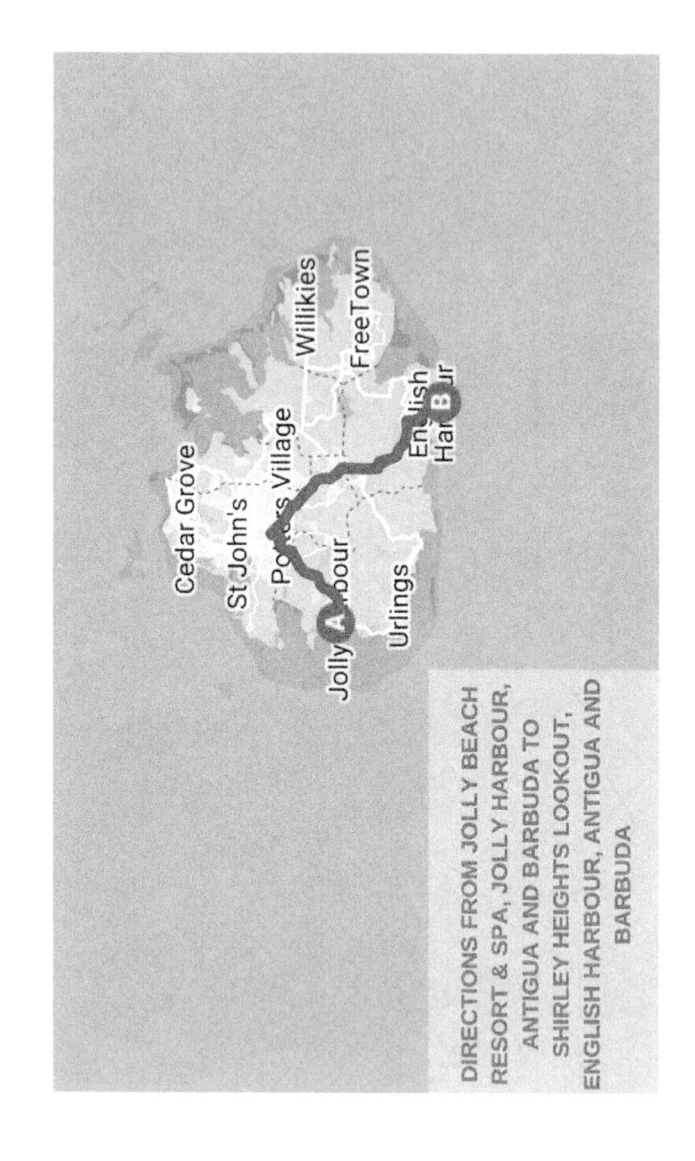

DIRECTIONS FROM JOLLY BEACH RESORT & SPA, JOLLY HARBOUR, ANTIGUA AND BARBUDA TO SHIRLEY HEIGHTS LOOKOUT, ENGLISH HARBOUR, ANTIGUA AND BARBUDA

DIRECTIONS FROM JOLLY BEACH RESORT & SPA, JOLLY HARBOUR, ANTIGUA AND BARBUDA TO NELSON'S DOCKYARD, DOCKYARD DRIVE, ANTIGUA AND BARBUDA

DIRECTIONS FROM JOLLY BEACH RESORT & SPA, JOLLY HARBOUR, ANTIGUA AND BARBUDA TO DARKWOOD BEACH, ANTIGUA AND BARBUDA

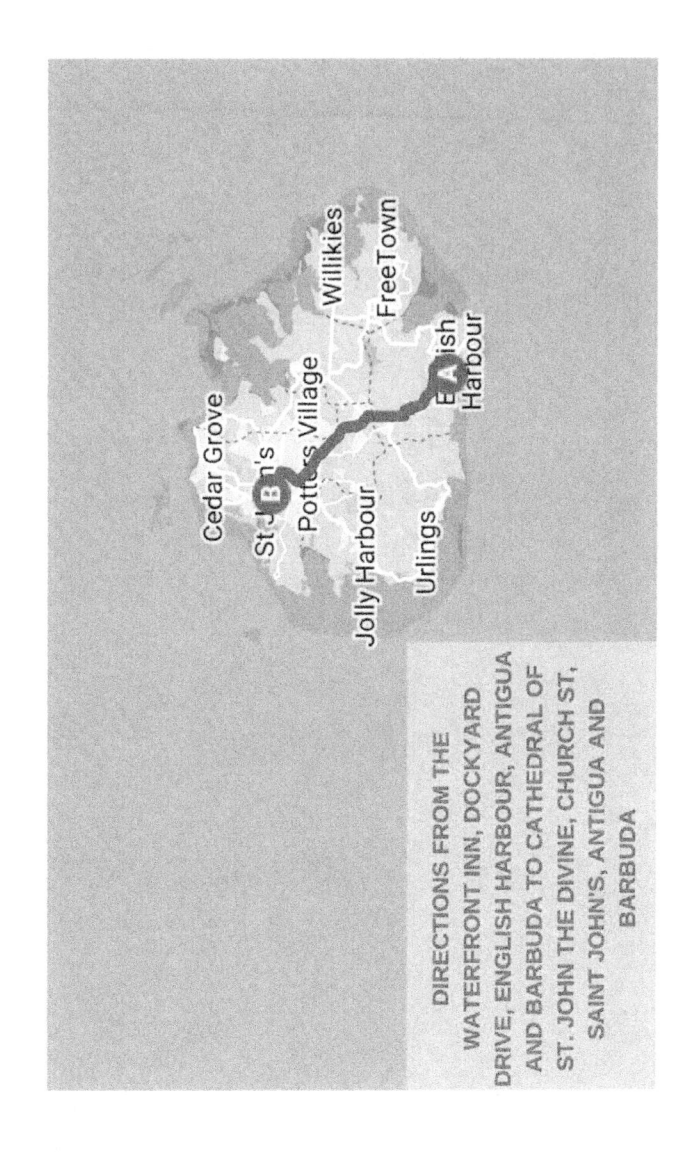

DIRECTIONS FROM THE WATERFRONT INN, DOCKYARD DRIVE, ENGLISH HARBOUR, ANTIGUA AND BARBUDA TO CATHEDRAL OF ST. JOHN THE DIVINE, CHURCH ST, SAINT JOHN'S, ANTIGUA AND BARBUDA

DIRECTIONS FROM THE WATERFRONT INN, DOCKYARD DRIVE, ENGLISH HARBOUR, ANTIGUA AND BARBUDA TO ANTIGUA RAIN FOREST CANOPY TOUR, FIG TREE DRIVE, ANTIGUA AND BARBUDA

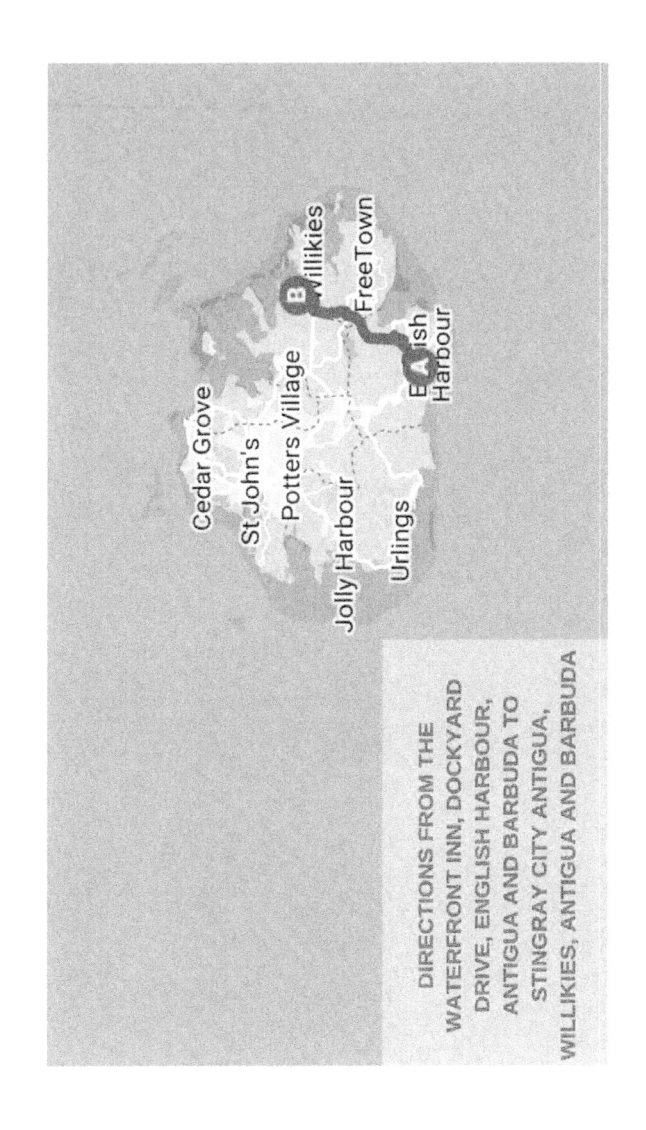

Willikies
FreeTown
English Harbour
Cedar Grove
St John's
Potters Village
Jolly Harbour
Urlings

DIRECTIONS FROM THE WATERFRONT INN, DOCKYARD DRIVE, ENGLISH HARBOUR, ANTIGUA AND BARBUDA TO STINGRAY CITY ANTIGUA, WILLIKIES, ANTIGUA AND BARBUDA

Printed in Great Britain
by Amazon